TOGAF® is NOT an EA Framework

The Inconvenient Pragmatic Truth

Kevin Lee Smith

Published by:
Pragmatic EA Ltd
25 Buttermere
Great Notley,
Essex CM77 7UY
England
http://www.PragmaticEA.com

First published:
May 2018
ISBN 978-1-908424-65-5 (hardback
ISBN 978-1-908424-66-2 (paperback)
ISBN 978-1-908424-67-9 (ebook)
© **Pragmatic** EA 2018

Other Titles in the Family:

Book	ISBN	Pre-requisites
PF2 The Pragmatic Family of Frameworks	978-1-908424-42-6	
Enterprise Direction A Pragmatic Approach using POED	978-1-908424-16-7	PF2
Enterprise Operation A Pragmatic Approach using POEO	978-1-908424-19-8	PF2
Enterprise Transformation A Pragmatic Approach using POET	978-1-908424-07-5	PF2
Enterprise Architecture A Pragmatic Approach using PEAF	978-1-908424-10-5	POET
Enterprise Engineering A Pragmatic Approach using PEEF	978-1-908424-13-6	POET
Enterprise Support A Pragmatic Approach using POES	978-1-908424-22-8	PF2
Enterprise Debt™ A Pragmatic Approach to Enterprise Transformation Governance	978-1-908424-48-8	
Enterprise Architecture Tools A Pragmatic Approach to EA Tool Selection and Adoption	978-1-908424-54-9	
What is EA A Pragmatic Explanation	978-1-908424-57-0	
The Culture of Enterprise Transformation The Inconvenient Pragmatic Truth	978-1-908424-59-4	
Enterprise Transformation Maturity Canvas A Pragmatic Approach to Maturity Assessment	978-1-908424-63-1	
TOGAF is NOT an EA Framework The Inconvenient Pragmatic Truth	978-1-908424-66-2	

"We cannot solve our problems,
with the same thinking we used when we created them."
Albert Einstein

"Sometimes it is the people who no one imagines anything of,
who do the things that no one can imagine."
Alan Turing

"Computers are useless.
They can only give you answers"
Pablo Picasso.

"You cannot 'cost justify' Architecture"
J. A. Zachman

"We have seen the enemy,
and the enemy is us (management)."
W. E. Deming

"If I have seen further,
it is by standing on the shoulders of giants."
Isaac Newton

Contents

Contributors

The author would like to acknowledge the contributors to this book.

Svyatoslav Kotusev

RMIT University
Kotusev@Kotusev.Com
Australia

Tom Graves

Tetradian Ltd
Tom@Tetradian.Com
Www.Tetradian.Com
UK

Orest Roman Swystun

Superlative Technologies
Orestswystun@Gmail.Com
USA

Kevin Lee Smith

Thinker
Pragmatic Ea Ltd
Kevin@Pragmaticea.Com
Www.Pragmaticea.Com
UK

Bouateli Abdenour

Enterprise Architect
Abouateli@Icloud.Com
France

Graham Berrisford

Managing Director
Avancier Ltd
Http://Avancier.Website
UK

INTRODUCTION

Basic Terminology

First let's get some terminology clear, straight out of the box:

Enterprise

An Enterprise is defined as a general noun, used to refer to things such as Public and Private Companies, Government Agencies, Charities, Universities etc. This is not an exhaustive list but illustrates the point. In addition, we use the word Enterprise as a general noun in place of many other words people may use to refer to each these "types". For example, a Private Company may be referred to as a Company, Business, Corporation, Conglomerate, Organisation, SME, Firm, Establishment, Group, Multinational or Venture.

Enterprise Architecture (noun)

Enterprise Architecture (noun) aka "**The Enterprise Architecture**", is defined as: The fundamental structure of an Enterprise, set in its context.

Enterprise Architecture (verb)

Enterprise Architecture (verb) aka "**Doing Enterprise Architecture**", is defined as all the work that must be done BEFORE an Enterprise starts executing transformation/change programmes, projects and initiatives, and the governance of those transformation/change programmes, projects and initiatives as they execute, in order to expose where they divert from the defined structural and transformation roadmaps, so appropriate business decisions can be made, to either allow the deviation and accept the consequences of doing so, or making changes so that the deviation is arrested.

Framework

A Framework exists to improve the way something is done (i.e. to increase the effectiveness and efficiency and to reduce the risk of failure). In many respects they are an expression of "Best Practice". They contain different types of things depending upon the purpose of the framework - its domain. More specifically, Frameworks are composed of information relating to at least one of these categories:

- **Methods** (e.g. processes, practices, etc) and/or
- **Artefacts** (e.g. Ontologies, Metamodels, Reference Models, Product Descriptions etc) and/or
- **Culture** (e.g. People, Culture, Values, Psychology, etc) and/or
- **Environment** (e.g. Tools, Frameworks, etc)

In addition, a framework may also contain information relating to:

- **Context** (How the Framework relates to the wider context of the domain and therefore defines the domain of the framework)
- **Adoption** (How the Framework can be adopted)

Some frameworks contain all of the above (e.g POET and PEAF).

Some frameworks contain some of the above (e.g TOGAF has no information on Context, Culture or Adoption).

Some frameworks contain only one of the above (e.g. Zachman is only an Ontology - an Artefact).

Many people take the view that a framework consists of only Artefact - meta-models, meta-meta-models (ontology), reference models, etc. This is a very engineering and IT myopic view.

However, this is plainly not true.

There are legal Frameworks, political Frameworks, cultural Frameworks, analysis Frameworks, architectural Frameworks, management Frameworks, business Frameworks, project management Frameworks, software development Frameworks, governance Frameworks, modelling Frameworks, etc, etc, etc. They may or may not have some information relating to meta-models or meta-meta-models or ontologies etc, but they are all frameworks - even the ones with no meta-model.

Why was this Book Compiled?

OK – so this is going to be a controversial book. Well – either that or it will be a largely ignored book. I know which one I would prefer 😉

Why do I see it necessary to denigrate a "competitor" – isn't that bad business practice?

Here are some comments I have received when looking for people who wished to be involved...

> "I assume the introduction covers why this is such an important debate? I'm not losing sleep over it as in the real world we have to adapt and draw upon all available resources. But your style turns me off somewhat. Let's talk about why we need something different rather than banging on about how wrong TOGAF is"

> "This is a foolish endeavour, that will be of little value to the practice of enterprise architecting."

But there are comments on the other side too...

> "In my decade of working as an architect for Accenture, Capgemini and Deloitte, I never heard anything but scorn for TOGAF. Even at Cap where many of the authors work, none of the real client-facing architects paid it any more than lip service."

> "I deleted it (a comment on LinkedIn) a few minutes after posting because although I know TOGAF as a destructive force I felt, after reflection, that particular thread perhaps wasn't the right place, for me, to make that comment. I tend to be more reserved in what I say as I feel that I have a brand to protect and don't want to be too contentious."

So, why did I decide to compile this book.

I believe that TOGAF has done more to damage the EA "profession" (such as it isn't!) than anything else in the world, and that the EA "profession" would be in a much better place today if TOGAF had never existed.

There are two main confusions that exist with regards to peoples (practitioners and management) understanding of EA.

1) Most people (90% perhaps) think that "it's all about IT".
2) Most people (90% perhaps) think that its all about running (mostly large) IT projects.

And the reason for this mass misunderstanding is because this is what TOGAF tends to push. People are told that TOGAF is an EA framework by the confused majority and so new people believe it to, which of course, adds to the majority thinking and saying the same wrong things.

These fundamental misunderstandings have to be tackled if an EA profession is to exist.

I compiled this book to start a proper debate on the subject and also to allow people to realise that there is a choice out there between which EA frameworks they can use and who they talk to that may have different ideas to The Open Group.

Why have so many people been on TOGAF training courses? I believe that everyone goes on TOGAF courses for 2 main reasons:

1) Because everyone else goes on TOGAF courses. (The herd mentality is strong and Nobody ever got fired for - hiring IBM / sending people on a TOGAF training course)
2) Because people do not know there is a choice. The market is saturated with companies and individuals selling TOGAF training courses (a google search of "+TOGAF +Training" returns over 400,000 results) and this saturation feed point 1 above.

But Kevin, there are many many people trained in TOGAF and many many Enterprises use it.

I certainly do not dispute the former. As of July 2017, The Open Group reported that the number of people Certified in TOGAF exceeds 70,00 in 134 countries. A great achievement indeed. But what benefit to Enterprises has that created.

My personal experience of Enterprise that "use" TOGAF is that most do not and those that say they do, on closer inspection, do not.

I have been employed by many enterprises specifically because I was TOGAF certified and that was mandatory, only to find out after much asking, that no one in the Enterprise used it or knew of anyone that used it in any way.

Are things improving.

The short answer is no.

I remember in the 80s and the 90s, and the 2000s that the number of projects failing was commonly referred to as around 70%. A huge figure.

Today, despite the apparent "takeup" of TOGAF, things do not appear to have changed:

- 70% of projects fail. [source: 4 PM]
- 60% of projects at IBM do not meet key goals (schedule, budget, and quality). [source: IBM]
- 17% of IT projects go so badly, they threaten the existence of the company. [source: McKinsey]
- 74% of all projects do not succeed. [source: PMI]
- 67% of all projects did not complete on time and on budget. [source: Standish Group]
- 75% of business and IT executives believe their projects are "doomed from the start." [source: Geneca]
- Only 2.5% of companies successfully complete 100% of their projects. [source: Gallup]
- High-performing organizations successfully complete 89% of their projects, while low performers complete only 36%. [source: PMI.org]
- Average cost overrun is 27%, but 17% had a cost overrun of 200% and a schedule overrun of 69%. [source: HBR]
- The failure rate of projects with budgets over $1M is 50% higher than the failure rate of projects with budgets below $350,000. [source: Gartner]
- 50% of all Project Management Offices [PMOs] close within just three years. [source: KeyedIN]
- 80% of project management executives don't know how their projects align with their company's business strategy. [source: Changepoint]
- Only 42% of organizations report having high alignment of projects to organizational strategy. [source: PMI]

https://tinyurl.com/yaeb78qr

It is not always easy to point out the Emperor is naked, or have opinions that conflict with the majority, but since the majority is wrong in a great many of instances, it is up to those brave souls who will stand up and say what they believe that will help to make the world a better place.

Progress does not come from echo chambers. Progress comes from debate and conflict.

I applaud the contributors to this book for standing up and poking their head above the parapet. Even if you do not agree with their views, I hope, at least, that you can agree with their commitment and right to do so and for their determination to stand up when many others cannot do so. Please take their voices as representative of far more people, that for whatever reasons (all valid) could not contribute due to worrying about the backlash.

https://tinyurl.com/ncqhnup

LEONARD FEHSKENS - THE OPEN GROUP

Sadly, Len passed away in 2017, but his words from a LinkedIn Discussion around 2014 are still pertinent to the debate. Len was also the sort of person who did not hide behind parapets. He is a great loss. Our thoughts are with his family.

Leonard (Len) Fehskens

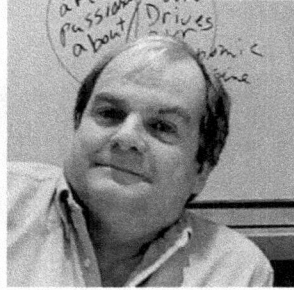

21 Feb 1947 – 29 August 2017

LinkedIn Comments

"TOGAF is clearly an EITA/EISA framework. The Open Group admits that, the TOGAF developers admit that. "

"Several people ask that The Open Group do something about TOGAF being mispositioned as an EA (rather than EISA or EITA) framework. We are. That's all I can say at this point. But, I have to remind you, there is a lot of inertia in the EA community, and while I am quite pleased that you all think TOGAF is so influential, just repositioning TOGAF properly is not going to change everyone's thinking overnight. I have been making the distinction between EA and EITA/EISA at every conference I have spoken at for at least five years now, and I feel rather more like Sisyphus than the kid who said the emperor has no clothes."

SVYATOSLAV KOTUSEV - RMIT

Enterprise Architecture Is Not TOGAF

By Svyatoslav Kotusev (RMIT)

Introduction

The Open Group Architecture Framework (TOGAF) is currently promoted as an industry consensus framework for enterprise architecture (EA) representing the best practice of numerous EA practitioners. However, my observations of successful companies using TOGAF as a basis for their EA efforts suggest that most TOGAF recommendations are usually found inapplicable, while the most critical parts of EA practice are usually established from scratch in company-specific ways. Therefore, my findings question the value of TOGAF as a standard for EA practice since successful TOGAF-based EA initiatives hardly overlap with the actual TOGAF prescriptions. More realistic and evidence-based sources on EA are needed.

The Value of TOGAF

In the recent years The Open Group Architecture Framework [1] has gained prominence as the most well-known framework for EA practice. It is positioned as an "open, industry consensus framework for enterprise architecture" [1, p. xxiii] representing the best practice of multiple companies practicing EA. Its core feature, Architecture Development Method (ADM), is "the result of continuous contributions from a large number of architecture practitioners" [1, p. 45]. Unsurprisingly, TOGAF is heavily promoted by various consultancies, experts and trainers. Is it really so valuable for organizations? Does it really reflect the best practice of successful organizations using EA?

My observations of leading Australian companies that wished to remain anonymous suggest negative answers to these questions. Although these companies use TOGAF as the key EA framework (one of them is even included in the "official" list of TOGAF users on The Open Group website, see The Open Group [2]), their actual activities hardly resemble TOGAF prescriptions. For instance, ADM - the core of TOGAF - is found inapplicable in practice and its steps are not followed in any of these companies. Similarly, other essential TOGAF features, including the Architecture Content Framework and Enterprise Continuum, are also not used in companies "using" TOGAF. Instead of following the step-wise and iterative ADM they established idiosyncratic sets of continuous EA-related processes. Instead of developing heaps of EA artifacts recommended by the Architecture Content Framework they established small pragmatic sets of value-adding documents with clearly defined aims, stakeholders and purpose. Consequently, the most critical parts of TOGAF-based EA initiatives were essentially "invented" from scratch in unique company-specific ways. On the other hand, useful TOGAF features adopted in these companies, such as four EA domains or architecture principles, are not really TOGAF-specific but rather conventional and have been used for decades [3, 4, 5]. Therefore, the core parts of TOGAF were found largely useless, useful parts of TOGAF were not TOGAF-specific, while the most critical parts of EA practice were established from scratch.

In light of these findings the growing popularity of TOGAF can hardly be attributed to the real usefulness of its advice, but rather to a lack of any better alternative sources on EA. This conclusion supports the opinion of Bloomberg [6, p. 1] that "TOGAF's accelerating success is simply because it's the only game in town" and that "TOGAF has gained traction simply because it's better than doing nothing". Despite the fact that many TOGAF recommendations are considered as overly complex and largely unrealistic, it still remains the most comprehensive available source on EA where some useful ideas can be found, while other EA frameworks are even less helpful. Consequently, the choice between TOGAF and other EA frameworks is essentially the choice between something and nothing, bad and very bad, largely useless and totally useless.

Although TOGAF is briskly discussed, heavily promoted and its certifications are required for enterprise architects at many companies, my findings suggest that successful EA efforts, even TOGAF-based, are built on pragmatic common sense ideas and rarely resemble the actual TOGAF recommendations. Therefore, TOGAF is used, arguably, more as a symbol than as a realistic actionable guidance. Following TOGAF does not guarantee a successful EA practice to an organization and getting TOGAF-certified does not guarantee a successful career to an EA practitioner. In short, TOGAF does not define EA practice, successful EA is not TOGAF.

New Sources for EA are Needed

Despite the promise that "TOGAF provides a best practice framework for adding value" [1, p. 7], the analysis of its usage shows that this best practice can be hardly applicable and TOGAF can be hardly used in any real sense: only as a "dictionary" where some useful information can occasionally be found or as a "horoscope" which vague recommendations can be adapted and interpreted to fit all organizations, however, not providing real practicable guidance to any of them. Though positioned as a comprehensive end-to-end EA framework covering most parts of EA practice, TOGAF rarely provides useful advice on its most critical aspects.

Surprisingly, my conclusions are not innovative and far from new but rather old and widely known. They are supported by numerous previous empirical studies [7, 8, 9, 10, 11, 12] that consistently demonstrate that EA frameworks, including TOGAF, have only a minor value at best or are even detrimental at worst. Consequently, this article is not a breakthrough but yet another reminder that successful EA initiatives have not much to do with the popular EA frameworks that are, arguably, no more than a typical *management fad* since their value is more than questionable. "Frameworks are cocaine for executives - they give them a huge rush and then they move to the next framework" [13, p. 1].

Therefore, I argue that the EA community should take a sober realistic look at existing EA literature, critically revise and rethink its idealistic ideas that are presently very distant from the real-world EA practice in organizations. New evidence-based comprehensive sources on EA are desperately needed as a substitute for largely useless but aggressively promoted EA frameworks.

References

[1] TOGAF (2011) "TOGAF Version 9.1" (#G116), The Open Group.

[2] The Open Group (2016) "TOGAF Users by Market Sector", The Open Group, URL: http://web.archive.org/web/20151121161238/http://www.opengroup.org/togaf/users-by-market-sector.

[3] PRISM (1986) "PRISM: Dispersion and Interconnection: Approaches to Distributed Systems Architecture", Cambridge, MA: CSC Index.

[4] Davenport, T. H., Hammer, M. and Metsisto, T. J. (1989) "How Executives Can Shape Their Company's Information Systems", *Harvard Business Review*, Vol. 67, No. 2, pp. 130-134.

[5] Richardson, G. L., Jackson, B. M. and Dickson, G. W. (1990) "A Principles-Based Enterprise Architecture: Lessons from Texaco and Star Enterprise", *MIS Quarterly*, Vol. 14, No. 4, pp. 385-403.

[6] Bloomberg, J. (2014) "Enterprise Architecture: Don't Be a Fool with a Tool", Forbes, URL: http://www.forbes.com/sites/jasonbloomberg/2014/08/07/enterprise-architecture-dont-be-a-fool-with-a-tool/.

[7] Buckl, S., Ernst, A. M., Lankes, J., Matthes, F. and Schweda, C. M. (2009) "State of the Art in Enterprise Architecture Management", Munich, Germany: Software Engineering for Business Information Systems (SEBIS).

[8] Smith, H. A., Watson, R. T. and Sullivan, P. (2012) "Delivering an Effective Enterprise Architecture at Chubb Insurance", *MIS Quarterly Executive*, Vol. 11, No. 2, pp. 75-85.

[9] Ross, J. W., Weill, P. and Robertson, D. C. (2006) *Enterprise Architecture as Strategy: Creating a Foundation for Business Execution*, Boston, MA: Harvard Business School Press.

[10] Ahlemann, F., Stettiner, E., Messerschmidt, M. and Legner, C. (eds.) (2012) *Strategic Enterprise Architecture Management: Challenges, Best Practices, and Future Developments*, Berlin: Springer.

[11] Haki, M. K., Legner, C. and Ahlemann, F. (2012) "Beyond EA Frameworks: Towards an Understanding of the Adoption of Enterprise Architecture Management", In: Pries-Heje, J., Chiasson, M., Wareham, J., Busquets, X., Valor, J. and Seiber, S. (eds.) *Proceedings of the 20th European Conference on Information Systems*, Barcelona, Spain: Association for Information Systems, pp. 1-12.

[12] Holst, M. S. and Steensen, T. W. (2011) "The Successful Enterprise Architecture Effort", *Journal of Enterprise Architecture*, Vol. 7, No. 4, pp. 16-22.

[13] Bloomberg, J. (2014) "Is Enterprise Architecture Completely Broken?", Forbes, URL: http://www.forbes.com/sites/jasonbloomberg/2014/07/11/is-enterprise-architecture-completely-broken/.

The Critical Scrutiny of TOGAF

By Svyatoslav Kotusev (RMIT University)

Introduction

In my previous article [1] I reported that The Open Group Architecture Framework (TOGAF) [2], the most comprehensive and widely known enterprise architecture (EA) framework, is largely of symbolic value and essentially has nothing to do with a successful EA practice. Unsurprisingly, the article provoked numerous comments from its readers ranging from full agreements to total disagreements and even direct insults. Therefore, I feel obliged to clarify several critically important points regarding TOGAF and its relationship to real EA practice. Observations in this article are my personal opinions based on an extensive EA literature analysis as well as on my studies of more than two dozen Australian and international companies with varying degrees of relationship to TOGAF. Two of these companies are included in the official TOGAF list [3], some of these companies claim to be TOGAF-based, some of them simply used TOGAF as a source of knowledge on EA, while others are largely indifferent to TOGAF.

Is TOGAF a Consistent Methodology or Just a Toolkit?

TOGAF community members currently position TOGAF as a useful toolkit for EA practice where necessary tools can be found. I argue that *TOGAF was originally designed as a consistent methodology, but was subsequently repositioned to a toolkit since de facto it can be useful at best as a toolkit.* For example, its original documentation clearly states that "[TOGAF] is a framework - a detailed method and a set of supporting tools - for developing an enterprise architecture" [2, p. 3]. The TOGAF Architecture Development Method (ADM) is "a step-by-step approach to develop and use an enterprise architecture" [2, p. 21] that "describes a method for developing and managing the lifecycle of an enterprise architecture" [2, p. 45], "defines a recommended sequence for the various phases and steps involved in developing an architecture" [2, p. 56] and "forms the core of TOGAF" [2, p. 45]. The TOGAF Architecture Content Framework (ACF) is "a detailed model of the outputs to be created by the ADM" [2, p. 37] that provides "a detailed open standard for how architectures should be described" [2, p. 34] and "a structural model for architectural content that allows the major work products that an architect creates to be consistently defined, structured, and presented" [2, p. 327]. "The ADM describes what needs to be done to create an architecture and the content framework describes what the architecture should look like once it is done" [2, p. 330]. At the same time, the word "toolkit" or similar definitions are never mentioned in the TOGAF documentation. Therefore, the original TOGAF documentation clearly describes TOGAF as a consistent methodology for EA practice describing both the processes that should be followed and the documents that should be produced as an output, not merely as a toolkit.

What is observed in real EA practice? I have never seen or heard of anybody who followed recommended ADM steps in any real sense or created a significant portion of documents recommended by the ACF. Architects unanimously complain that these recommendations are too rigid and impractical. Instead architects typically developed 8-12 different documents hardly overlapping with the ACF and followed no specific iterative processes resembling the ADM. Similar findings are reported by other authors as well. "Our initial assumptions about TOGAF were that it would be a sort of 'methodology' that we could follow to produce our EA, however this turned out not to be the case" [4, p. 63]. "Our views on TOGAF inevitably changed as the project progressed. Working sequentially through the TOGAF [ADM] cycle ceased to make sense" [4, p. 48]. Consequently, TOGAF was originally designed as "a detailed method and a set of supporting tools" [2, p. 3], but has been later repositioned by the TOGAF community to be merely a "set of supporting tools" since its "detailed method" proved absolutely impractical.

Interestingly, the word "Framework" in its title was also repositioned accordingly from its original to a new meaning. The notion of EA framework seemingly was originally introduced by the PRISM framework [5, 6] and then widely popularized by the Zachman Framework [7]. In these early days an EA framework was defined as "a logical structure for classifying and organizing the descriptive representations of an Enterprise" [8, p. 2]. Even TOGAF officially defines an architecture framework as "a conceptual structure used to develop, implement, and sustain an architecture" [2, p. 21]. However, TOGAF-certified EA practitioners report that their trainers now interpret the word "Framework" in its title as "a set of reusable components", in a meaning similar to which it is used in Ruby on Rails, Spring, CakePHP and other application frameworks, but which is essentially unrelated to its original meaning. Therefore, not only TOGAF was repositioned from a methodology to a toolkit, but even the word "Framework" in its title was also re-imbued with a new meaning to denote "a set of reusable components" instead of "a structure for describing enterprises".

Is TOGAF Really Based on Best Practice?

EA practitioners often believe that TOGAF is based on an industry best practice in EA developed by *some other* successful companies. It is not surprising taking into account the claims of The Open Group that "TOGAF has been developed through the collaborative efforts of over 300 Architecture Forum member companies from some of the world's leading companies and organizations" [2, p. 7] and "provides a best practice framework for adding value" [2, p. 7].

However, if nobody follows ADM steps or develops the heaps of recommended EA documents, then whose best practice is it? I have never seen any architects or organizations who might have said that the ADM, ACF or Enterprise Continuum represent their *actual* best practice. Most EA practitioners I have spoken to agree that these recommendations can hardly be based on real best practice, while others opine that their organizations are merely "not mature enough yet" for this best practice. But here I want to notice that TOGAF appeared in 1995 and its core elements, for instance the ADM, remain virtually unchanged since then. How can it be that someone's best practice developed more than 20 years ago still cannot be implemented anywhere because organizations are "not mature enough yet"? Moreover, TOGAF is based on the Technical Architecture Framework for Information Management (TAFIM) [9], but TAFIM was reportedly retired as unsuccessful because EA projects required huge investments of time and money, resulting architectures were often obsolete before the completion and business stakeholders were usually unable to understand them [10, 11]. If TOGAF is based on TAFIM and TAFIM proved unsuccessful, then how can TOGAF be based on best practice?

In the light of these observations it becomes clear that TOGAF reflect nobody's actual best practice, while the real origin of its core recommendations remains largely obscure. At the same time, the promises of The Open Group that TOGAF "provides a best practice framework" [2, p. 7] can be considered only as typical meaningless marketing statements aiming to promote the product sales unsurprisingly coming from the TOGAF's vendor and the motivation behind them is perfectly clear. For instance, there is currently more than 52 thousand TOGAF-certified individuals worldwide [12]. It means that The Open Group has earned at least 23 million dollars on TOGAF certifications only [13]. If you add various trainings, courses, books, conferences, consulting and other lucrative TOGAF-related services provided by The Open Group, then this number will probably be much bigger. If you were The Open Group, would not you claim that TOGAF represents best practice?

Therefore, the conclusion here is pretty unambiguous: core TOGAF recommendations do not represent (and never represented) anybody's actual best practice, but rather came from some other unclear sources.

Is Actual Best Practice Reflected in TOGAF?

Although it is clear that main TOGAF recommendations did not originate from real best practice, another question from the opposite perspective is to what extent real best practice is reflected in TOGAF. In other words, is actual best practice at least a subset of TOGAF?

My analysis of actual EA-related activities in the studied organizations suggests that real best practice is hardly included in TOGAF. Probably the most prominent example demonstrating this conclusion is the EA artefact typically called the Business Capability Map/Model (BCM) [14, 15, 16], which is widely used in the vast majority of the studied organizations, but is not even mentioned in TOGAF at all. In fact, the BCM plays a very significant role in EA practices of many organizations and has numerous beneficial applications. For instance: (1) heatmapping – identifying strategically important capabilities and focusing IT investments there, (2) footprinting – mapping different IT solutions to capabilities in order to compare their business value, (3) determining impact – mapping an IT project to capabilities in order to understand how it will affect the business, (4) identifying stakeholders - mapping an IT project to capabilities in order to identify its stakeholders, (5) predicting disruption - mapping an IT project to capabilities in order to understand which activities may be disrupted, (6) scoping - mapping an IT project to capabilities in order to its overall scope, (7) the BCM provides a common organization-wide vocabulary and a reference model for various stakeholders to facilitate communication. Therefore, the use of BCM is evidently a part of actual best practice in EA. However, ~700 pages TOGAF document describes neither the BCM itself nor its numerous applications. Moreover, a brief analysis of the release notes of TOGAF Version 9.1 [2, p. 35] suggests that TOGAF is not even moving towards real industry best practice.

Consequently, real best practice essentially is not included in TOGAF, i.e. TOGAF hardly overlaps with actual best practice in EA.

Is TOGAF Flexible?

TOGAF community members typically argue that TOGAF should be adapted before use and often praise TOGAF for its flexibility since it can be tailored to fit numerous situations and organizations. But where are the limits of this flexibility? In other words, to what extent can TOGAF be adapted and yet remain TOGAF?

Interestingly, TOGAF used to give an answer to this question. Section 2.11 of TOGAF Version 9 ("TOGAF Document Categorization Model") [17, p. 18] classified the content of TOGAF into core, mandated, recommended and supporting sections. Core sections are "the fundamental concepts that form the essence of TOGAF" [17, p. 18], while mandated sections are "the normative parts of the TOGAF specification" that "are central to its usage and without them the framework would not be recognizably TOGAF" [17, p. 18]. All the key elements of TOGAF, including ADM phases, Architecture Deliverables and Enterprise Continuum, are classified as either core or mandated meaning that the officially-defined use of TOGAF implies using ADM phases *and* Architecture Deliverables *and* Enterprise Continuum. Since I have never seen or heard of any organizations using *any* of these elements in any real sense, it can be safely stated that probably nobody on this planet uses TOGAF at all. Unsurprisingly, the release notes of TOGAF Version 9.1 inform readers that "the Document Categorization Model has been removed" [2, p. 36] and, therefore, now any EA-related activities can be interpreted as "using adapted TOGAF" and described as "TOGAF-based" regardless of their relationship to the actual TOGAF recommendations. Whatever you do, you use TOGAF.

However, what is much more important is that nobody I am aware of is able to articulate clearly how exactly TOGAF should be adapted. TOGAF's ~700 pages documentation mentions the need for adaptation, but does not answer the question "How exactly?" either. I argue that *the recommendation to adapt TOGAF without specifying how exactly is an evident logical trick, "catch-22"*.

Consider the following recommendation clearly illustrating the typical deceitful TOGAF-style pattern: "To eat your soup you should use (1) a fork or (2) any other instrument". This recommendation looks utterly nonsensical because (1) eating soup with a fork is obviously impractical but (2) the advice to use any other instrument does not convey any information at all. Consequently, the value of this recommendation is negative or nil. Looking through the TOGAF lenses this recommendation can be read as: "To practice EA you should follow (1) ADM steps or (2) any other processes". Here again (1) following ADM steps is obviously impractical but (2) the advice to follow any other processes does not convey any information at all. In fact, TOGAF is abundant in similar recommendations where (1) doing what is recommended is obviously impractical but (2) the suggestion to adapt this recommendation into something else is uninformative. Therefore, for most aspects of EA practice TOGAF is indeed flexible, i.e. does not prescribe anything in particular. As a result, TOGAF-certified EA practitioners are free to do whatever they find reasonable and praise TOGAF for its flexibility since TOGAF generously allows them to adapt (actually ignore) its own unreasonable advice. Unreasonableness of TOGAF's advice is compensated by optionality of its execution.

This situation puts The Open Group in an extremely beneficial position, while the position of EA practitioners seems desperate. The position of The Open Group is essentially a "lossless lottery": any failures of TOGAF-based EA practices can be attributed to the improper adaptation of TOGAF's best practice recommendations by unqualified architects, while any successes of TOGAF-unrelated EA practices can be "appropriated" as TOGAF-based because TOGAF is very flexible and allows any behaviour. Since TOGAF allows any arbitrary adaptations, all successful EA practices can be considered TOGAF-based. This deceptive "flexibility trick" puts TOGAF beyond any critique: TOGAF is always good, you just need to adapt it properly (somehow). At the same time, EA practitioners have no one to blame but themselves: they are given "industry consensus EA best practice" by The Open Group and now it is their turn to adapt and use it properly.

Taking into account the previous conclusions that the TOGAF's advice is not best practice and that actual best practice is not included in TOGAF at all, very impressive flexibility is required in order to transform TOGAF into a working EA practice. Adapting TOGAF implies not only throwing away ADM, ACF and Enterprise Continuum, but also inventing something reasonable instead of them. From this perspective "using TOGAF" can be best explained as "studying TOGAF and then doing something else instead", and this is praised as TOGAF's flexibility.

Therefore, the conclusion here is again unequivocal: the admired flexibility of TOGAF is nothing more than a simple trick helping (1) conceal impracticality of the actual TOGAF's recommendations, (2) put the burden of responsibility for improper adaptation on EA practitioners, (3) avoid any potential criticism and (4) interpret successes and failures "properly".

What Is TOGAF?

Since TOGAF consists of ~700 pages of strange optional prescriptions of an unknown origin hardly overlapping with actual best practice in EA, it can be best described as *a toolkit of random EA-related recommendations*. Unsurprisingly, the value of TOGAF is also haphazard. It can only be realized if some of its random recommendations accidentally turn out useful, maybe yes, maybe no. For instance, EA practitioners, though unanimously opine that TOGAF cannot be used as a consistent EA methodology, still admit that TOGAF can have some value. However, different EA practitioners find different random fragments of TOGAF valuable and these fragments are typically of secondary importance: some people find the idea of building blocks useful, some the idea of a viewpoint, technical reference model or some deliverables from some phases. Moreover, since TOGAF offers nothing in particular except the flexibility to "pick whatever you want, adapt it as you wish and use it any way you like", it is *fundamentally unable to provide any meaningful, systematic and consistent description of EA and EA practice*. As a result, regardless of how well you know TOGAF, it is arguably impossible to establish a successful EA practice from scratch if you have never seen previously how successful EA practices look like and work in other organizations. For instance, one interviewee compared the EA profession to a craftsmen's guild where the only way to acquire the necessary skills is to become an apprentice and learn from your master.

TOGAF can be also described as *a distractor of attention* because it draws the discourse in the EA community away from real EA-related questions. In other words, people discuss TOGAF instead of discussing EA (with this article being the brightest illustration of this statement). Instead of EA education we get TOGAF certification. Instead of asking right questions, for instance "What works?" and "What does not work?", many EA practitioners tend to ask artificial questions, for instance "How should TOGAF be properly applied?", "What are the advantages of TOGAF?" or "What is better, TOGAF or Zachman?". All these TOGAF-inspired questions do not make much sense and cannot advance our understanding of EA. Unfortunately, the academic EA community is fascinated with TOGAF as well. Significant efforts are put into the scientific analysis of TOGAF [18, 19, 20, 21] instead of empirical EA practice. Moreover, the situation in academe from this perspective is probably much worse than among EA practitioners, since many "paper" researchers live in their theoretical ivory towers and hardly understand the existence of a gap between EA theory and practice. For instance, the first version of my paper intended to study the practical usage of EA artefacts [22] was rejected by an anonymous reviewer with the following comment (among others): "Frameworks such as TOGAF provide very detailed instructions for their users in terms of methodology and [artefacts]. I do not see the value of redefining these". More interestingly, the presence of TOGAF in the EA discourse generates the phenomenon of "doublethink" - simultaneous acceptance of two mutually contradictory beliefs as correct. For instance, the question "Do we know something about EA practice?" typically gets answered with "Yes, TOGAF is a widely-accepted comprehensive industry standard defining EA practice", but the question "Can TOGAF be interpreted literally and followed step-by-step to practice EA?" typically gets answered with "No, TOGAF is only a framework, it should be modified (somehow) for specific organizations". In this situation we supposedly know much about EA practice because TOGAF exists, but at the same time we also do not know anything about EA practice because nobody can specify how exactly TOGAF should be used. Consequently, the existence of TOGAF suggests that we *know much* and *do not know anything* about EA practice at the same time. This doublethink essentially leads to a dead end in the EA discipline because EA studies neither can be started from scratch (because TOGAF exists), nor can be based on TOGAF (because it is not clear how exactly it is used). Therefore, the existence of

TOGAF only wastes our time and inhibits rather than facilitates our progress in real understanding of EA.

What is more surprising, TOGAF can be considered essentially as *a religious text* due to the following properties: (1) its real origin and authorship are disputable, (2) it offers the wisdom of a mythical origin, (3) it cannot be understood literally, but needs to be properly interpreted, (4) it is promoted by enlightened gurus who know how to construe it, (5) when properly interpreted, it has answers to all questions, (6) its original text does not change, while its interpretations evolve and (7) it is vague enough to be universal. Consider the following supernatural description of TOGAF at work by a well-known TOGAF guru: "Organizations start with an open framework like the TOGAF framework, but as it gets customized and tailored, it adapts to an organization's culture to become their own "personalized" enterprise architecture model. As enterprise architecture matures in an organization, the TOGAF framework is still inside and powering their enterprise architecture but no longer very visible" [23, p. 16]. If it is not a sermon, then what is it?

This religious nature of TOGAF has *very* important implications for the discourse around it. Firstly, EA practitioners converted in TOGAF faith will be always convinced that they use TOGAF whatever they do regardless of any logical arguments against it, even if they actually do not follow a single recommendation out of it. Secondly, whether to be or not to be TOGAF-based is only a matter of a personal conviction. For instance, I have met some faithful TOGAF believers who seemingly never read its original text, but only visited some courses where gurus explained them how to interpret and use TOGAF "properly". Therefore, many people believe they use TOGAF without being aware of what exactly the original TOGAF text says. As a result, *many people are convinced that EA practice is TOGAF*, which is not so [1]. This fact that many people learn TOGAF only from gurus, but never read its original text explains how TOGAF could be effortlessly reinterpreted and repositioned from a methodology to merely a toolkit *even without modifying its original text*. Thirdly, arguments around TOGAF might be interesting and might even spark "religious wars", but they are utterly useless and make no difference at all. Fourthly, TOGAF lives in people's hearts, not brains. Therefore, regardless of any future evidence-based scientific progress in our understanding of EA, TOGAF's text will not change (but its interpretations still may change) and TOGAF's congregation will not decline. As world religions can exist in parallel with physics, chemistry and biology, TOGAF can also exist in parallel with evidence-based sources on EA [24, 25], which are typically inconsistent with TOGAF. Regardless of any possible criticism, no matter how substantiated, TOGAF will stay with us and remain a curious phenomenon of the EA world.

Why TOGAF Is So Popular?

I argue that the popularity of TOGAF can be attributed to three main factors. The first factor is the aggressive promotion of TOGAF. Numerous gurus, trainers, instructors, experts, consultants, certification centres etc. make their fortunes "selling" TOGAF. Unsurprisingly, all these parties are interested in promoting TOGAF and avoiding any criticism towards it. They are all working hard to support the image of TOGAF as a globally recognized de facto industry standard in EA based on best practice of world-leading companies. What is interesting here is that EA consultancies can sell their services under the TOGAF brand perfectly understanding its symbolic value. For instance, one of the few available evidence-based sources on EA [24] co-authored by PricewaterhouseCoopers (PwC) experts clearly suggests that successful EA practice has not much to do with TOGAF or any other EA frameworks, but yet PwC's website promises to provide "advice consistent with industry leading frameworks such as TOGAF and Zachman" [26].

The second factor is a lack of any serious alternatives to TOGAF. On the one hand, other promoted and well-known EA frameworks are even more useless for real EA practice than TOGAF and do not deserve any attention at all. On the other hand, other available reasonably good sources on EA [24, 25] are (1) not promoted and therefore are not well-known to "mass-readership", (2) not distributed for free, (3) not frameworks, while EA is strongly associated with frameworks and (4) not comprehensive. Consequently, for many EA practitioners the only visible alternative to TOGAF is the Zachman Framework and TOGAF turns out to be the lesser of two evils. Moreover, the situation here looks hopeless since probably nobody of powerful players on the EA market is motivated to propose any alternatives to TOGAF: if people willingly pay for TOGAF, then why invent something else?

The third factor is the shameful (or even criminal) inertness of the EA research community, which I belong to. Unfortunately, EA researchers generally do not provide any objective analysis of the situation in the EA discipline. As a result, trustworthy and evidence-based information on EA can hardly be found. In this atmosphere of ignorance numerous EA-related myths, legends and superstitions propagate very quickly. Due to a number of pretty complex reasons academic EA researchers are typically obsessed with producing "scientific" theories instead of answering real practical questions. Consequently, EA research rarely goes beyond paltry questions, like comparing EA frameworks or speculating on theoretical benefits of EA. There are more than a thousand of academic publications on EA, but this impressive heap of "knowledge" cannot answer even the simplest relevant questions, for instance which documents are typically used in EA practice and how. Therefore, the academic EA research community is essentially powerless and unable not only to propose some comprehensive alternatives to TOGAF, but even to restrain the propagation of dangerous TOGAF-related superstitions. The fact that TOGAF is now taught at the prestigious university [27] clearly demonstrates the capitulation of an academic army to marketing aggressors.

Conclusion

TOGAF is definitely an interesting phenomenon of the EA world because: (1) it is based on a methodology previously rejected as ineffective (TAFIM [9]), (2) it claims to be based on best practice, but is unable to provide any examples of successful implementation, (3) it gained enormous popularity, but brings only a minor random value, (4) it is closely associated with the notion of EA, but is unable to explain how EA works and even what EA is, (5) everybody knows that TOGAF should be adapted, but nobody can say how exactly, (6) it is successfully sold to very intelligent people with simplistic tricks, (7) people question its value, but are eager to get certified (I got my TOGAF certificate as well), (8) it claims to disseminate best practice, but actually inhibits its dissemination and (9) it acquired faithful believers.

Essentially, TOGAF is a toolkit of random EA-related recommendations which is unable to describe what EA practice is and even what EA is, but still can bring some accidental marginal value. To "use TOGAF" actually means to "study TOGAF and then do whatever you find reasonable" and, therefore, means nothing at all. The existence of TOGAF only distracts our attention and impedes our understanding of EA.

However, since TOGAF can be considered as a religious text and a freedom of religion is guaranteed by the constitution, everyone is free to believe in TOGAF, use TOGAF and find TOGAF valuable or even essential for EA practice. TOGAF faith cannot be prohibited, ridiculed or even condemned. Therefore, faithful TOGAF believers are free to stay content with metaphysical explanations of how TOGAF "adapts to an organization's culture to become their own "personalized" enterprise architecture model" and then is "powering their enterprise architecture but no longer very visible" [23], but all others feeling sceptical about vague TOGAF babble should forget TOGAF and study evidence-based sources on EA, of which two most important probably are "Enterprise Architecture as Strategy: Creating a Foundation for Business Execution" [25] and "Strategic Enterprise Architecture Management: Challenges, Best Practices, and Future Developments" [24].

References

[1] Kotusev, S. (2016) "Enterprise Architecture Is Not TOGAF", British Computer Society (BCS), URL: http://www.bcs.org/content/conWebDoc/55547.

[2] TOGAF (2011) "TOGAF Version 9.1" (#G116), The Open Group.

[3] The Open Group (2016) "TOGAF Users by Market Sector", The Open Group, URL: http://web.archive.org/web/20151121161238/http://www.opengroup.org/togaf/users-by-market-sector.

[4] Anderson, P., Backhouse, G., Townsend, J., Hedges, M. and Hobson, P. (2009) "Doing Enterprise Architecture: Enabling the Agile Institution" (#533), Bristol, The United Kingdom: Joint Information Systems Committee (JISC).

[5] PRISM (1986) "PRISM: Dispersion and Interconnection: Approaches to Distributed Systems Architecture", Cambridge, MA: CSC Index.

[6] Rivera, R. (2013) "The PRISM Architecture Framework - Was It the Very First Enterprise Architecture Framework?", *Journal of Enterprise Architecture*, Vol. 9, No. 4, pp. 14-18.

[7] Zachman, J. A. (1987) "A Framework for Information Systems Architecture", *IBM Systems Journal*, Vol. 26, No. 3, pp. 276-292.

[8] Zachman, J. A. (1996) "Concepts of the Framework for Enterprise Architecture: Background, Description and Utility", Monument, CO: Zachman International.

[9] TAFIM (1996) "Department of Defense Technical Architecture Framework for Information Management, Volume 4: DoD Standards-Based Architecture Planning Guide (Version 3.0)", Arlington County, VA: Defense Information Systems Agency.

[10] Goikoetxea, A. (2007) *Enterprise Architectures and Digital Administration: Planning, Design, and Assessment*, Singapore: World Scientific Publishing.

[11] Perks, C. and Beveridge, T. (2003) *Guide to Enterprise IT Architecture*, New York, NY: Springer.

[12] TOGAF (2016) "Directory of Certified People", The Open Group, URL: https://togaf9-cert.opengroup.org/certified-individuals.

[13] TOGAF (2016) "TOGAF Examination Fees", The Open Group, URL: https://togaf9-cert.opengroup.org/examination-fees.

[14] Scott, J. (2009) "Business Capability Maps: The Missing Link Between Business Strategy and IT Action", *Architecture and Governance Magazine*, Vol. 5, No. 9, pp. 1-4.

[15] Swindell, A. (2014) "Business Capability Models: Why You Might Be Missing Out on Better Business Outcomes", *Architecture and Governance Magazine*, Vol. 10, No. 2, pp. 3-7.

[16] Keller, W. (2015) "Using Capability Models for Strategic Alignment", In: Simon, D. and Schmidt, C. (eds.) *Business Architecture Management: Architecting the Business for Consistency and Alignment*, Berlin: Springer, pp. 107-122.

[17] TOGAF (2009) "TOGAF Version 9" (#G091), The Open Group.

[18] Dietz, J. L. and Hoogervorst, J. A. (2011) "A Critical Investigation of TOGAF - Based on the Enterprise Engineering Theory and Practice", In: Albani, A., Dietz, J. L. and Verelst, J. (eds.) *Advances in Enterprise Engineering V*, Berlin: Springer, pp. 76-90.

[19] Zadeh, M. E., Millar, G. and Lewis, E. (2012) "Mapping the Enterprise Architecture Principles in TOGAF to the Cybernetic Concepts - An Exploratory Study", In: Sprague, R. H. (ed.) *Proceedings of the 45th Hawaii International Conference on System Sciences*, Maui, HI: IEEE, pp. 4270-4276.

[20] Mueller, T., Schuldt, D., Sewald, B., Morisse, M. and Petrikina, J. (2013) "Towards Inter-Organizational Enterprise Architecture Management - Applicability of TOGAF 9.1 for Network Organizations", In: Shim, J. P., Hwang, Y. and Petter, S. (eds.) *Proceedings of the 19th Americas Conference on Information Systems*, Chicago, IL: Association for Information Systems, pp. 1-13.

[21] Alm, R. and Wißotzki, M. (2013) "TOGAF Adaption for Small and Medium Enterprises", In: Abramowicz, W. (ed.) *Proceedings of the 16th International Conference on Business Information Systems Workshops*, Poznan, Poland: Springer, pp. 112-123.

[22] Kotusev, S., Singh, M. and Storey, I. (2015) "Investigating the Usage of Enterprise Architecture Artifacts", In: Becker, J., vom Brocke, J. and de Marco, M. (eds.) *Proceedings of the 23rd European Conference on Information Systems*, Munster, Germany: Association for Information Systems, pp. 1-12.

[23] Viswanathan, V. (2015) "Four Questions: Vish Viswanathan", *Journal of Enterprise Architecture*, Vol. 11, No. 2, pp. 15-17.

[24] Ahlemann, F., Stettiner, E., Messerschmidt, M. and Legner, C. (eds.) (2012) *Strategic Enterprise Architecture Management: Challenges, Best Practices, and Future Developments*, Berlin: Springer.

[25] Ross, J. W., Weill, P. and Robertson, D. C. (2006) *Enterprise Architecture as Strategy: Creating a Foundation for Business Execution*, Boston, MA: Harvard Business School Press.

[26] PwC (2016) "Enterprise Architecture: Creating the Blueprint of Your Business", PricewaterhouseCoopers (PwC), URL: http://www.pwc.com/ca/en/services/consulting/technology/advisory/enterprise-architecture-governance.html.

[27] NUS (2016) "NICF - Certified Enterprise Architecture Practitioner Course", National University of Singapore, Institute of Systems Science, URL: https://www.iss.nus.edu.sg/ProfessionalCourses/SearchCourse/CourseDetail/tabid/267/cid/1/cname/nicf-certified-enterprise-architecture-practitioner-course/Default.aspx.

TOGAF: Just the Next Fad That Turned into a New Religion

By Svyatoslav Kotusev (RMIT University)

Introduction

Currently the discourse in the enterprise architecture (EA) discipline largely revolves around The Open Group Architecture Framework (TOGAF). TOGAF is actively promoted by many consultancies and gurus as a leading EA framework. For example, The Open Group claims that TOGAF is "a proven Enterprise Architecture methodology and framework" as well as "the most prominent and reliable Enterprise Architecture standard in the world" [1, p. 1]. TOGAF describes an EA practice as an iterative step-wise process consisting of eight consecutive phases where each of these phases produces a specified set of architectural deliverables. This iterative process is titled as TOGAF architecture development method (ADM) and implies describing the current state, defining the desired future state, analyzing the gaps between these states, developing a transition plan, executing the plan and then repeating the same process all over again. But what is the true origin of TOGAF ADM? Where did TOGAF really come from? What is TOGAF?

Just the Next Fad...

In fact, the historical roots of the sequential step-by-step planning process currently recommended by TOGAF ADM can be traced back to the earliest proposed approaches to information systems planning [2, 3] and especially to the Business Systems Planning (BSP) methodology initiated by IBM in the end of the 1960s [4, 5, 6]. These early information systems planning methodologies advocated approximately the same step-wise planning approach closely resembling TOGAF ADM and also recommended in some form or the other to analyze the current information systems support, create a comprehensive plan of required information systems and then develop and follow the roadmap for transition from the current state to the desired future state [7].

After the introduction of BSP, other consulting companies readily proposed their own BSP-like planning methodologies essentially representing slightly different variations of BSP. These methodologies included, among others, Method/1 promoted by Arthur Andersen (now Accenture), 4FRONT promoted by Deloitte & Touche (now Deloitte), Summit S promoted by Coopers & Lybrand (now part of PwC) and the analogous planning methodology promoted by Nolan, Norton & Company (now part of KPMG) [8, 9, 10]. Highly similar planning methodologies had been also proposed by individual consultants and gurus [11, 12, 13] and later even by U.S. government agencies [14, 15]. Although most of these methodologies used the newer and more fashionable term "architecture" in different variations, e.g. information systems architecture, and were positioned accordingly as architecture planning methodologies, all of them still advocated essentially the same old planning approach as BSP, i.e. understand the current architecture, develop the desired target architecture and compose the migration plan. Even the seminal BSP methodology itself in its later versions also switched from unfashionable information systems plans to more trendy architecture [16].

The next notable wave of architecture planning methodologies was Information Engineering. After being initially proposed by IBM alumni Clive Finkelstein and James Martin in 1981 [17, 18], Information Engineering eventually diverged into a number of distinct sub-streams and essentially became a broad umbrella term for a cohort of slightly different sibling methodologies promoted by various consultancies and gurus [19, 20, 21, 22], including James Martin's Strategic Data/Information Planning [23, 24]. Information Engineering had a strong data accent and emphasized the importance of data as the most stable element of information systems. Information Engineering recommended first to develop a solid information architecture, or data architecture, and only then to derive the structure of necessary information systems from this architecture. However, despite its primary focus on data, Information Engineering still recommended fundamentally the same step-wise planning approach as the original BSP methodology, i.e. developing a comprehensive ideal architecture, contrasting this architecture with the existing information systems and then creating a transition plan to implement the required architecture.

Finally, the current term "enterprise architecture" became in vogue. The first planning methodology referring to enterprise architecture called Enterprise Architecture Planning (EAP) advocated the same familiar BSP-like planning approach and even explicitly admitted that "EAP has its roots in IBM's BSP" [25, p. 53]. Later the EAP methodology provided the basis for the Federal Enterprise Architecture Framework (FEAF), one of the most well-known EA frameworks [26, pp. 20-22]. The fancy term "enterprise architecture" and its different variations, e.g. enterprise IT architecture or enterprise information architecture, had been willingly adopted by the broader consulting community. As a result, countless companies and gurus readily proposed their own EA methodologies and frameworks. This generation included, among others, the EA methodologies proposed by Bernard Boar [27],

Jaap Schekkerman [28] and Scott Bernard [29], the Department of Defense Architecture Framework (DoDAF) [30] and many other less prominent EA methodologies and frameworks [31, 32, 33, 34, 35, 36, 37, 38, 39, 40, 41]. Regardless of their apparent novelty, all these EA methodologies and frameworks essentially replicated the same decades-old planning approach inspired by BSP with minor deviations and also recommended to study the current state, describe the desired state, analyze the gaps and develop the roadmap in a very similar step-wise manner. Among these "new" EA frameworks was also TOGAF aggressively promoted by The Open Group [42]. TOGAF ADM is based on the earlier TAFIM architecture planning process [14], which was itself rooted in some previous architecture planning methodologies of the 1980s, and recommends exactly the same step-by-step planning methodology.

The brief historical analysis provided above clearly demonstrates that TOGAF as a planning approach *cannot be considered as new in any real sense*. For instance, virtually all phases, artifacts, deliverables, modeling techniques, architecture domains and other ideas that can be found in TOGAF had been actually proposed earlier by some of the numerous previous architecture-based planning methodologies. Put it simply, none of the core TOGAF ideas are really TOGAF-specific. Historically, TOGAF represents merely the next, rather recent methodology in the broader 50-years-old stream of various formal architecture-based planning methodologies promoted more or less successfully by different parties during different time periods from the 1960s to the present days. This stream gradually evolved through different epochs from information systems planning of the 1960s-1970s, to information systems architecture of the 1980s-1990s and finally to enterprise architecture of the 2000s-2010s. From this perspective, TOGAF can be considered only as one of many other similar "boats" flowing in the common "river" of architecture-based planning methodologies.

Despite the long historical evolution and considerable stylistic differences between various architecture-based methodologies, the overall planning approach, fundamental ideas and underlying assumptions of all these methodologies stayed largely unchanged through all these decades. Specifically, all architecture-based planning methodologies from BSP to TOGAF regardless of their specific titles, e.g. information systems plans or enterprise architecture, recommended essentially the same formal, top-down and step-wise planning approach, where each step produces certain deliverables providing an input for the subsequent steps. The high-level logic of all architecture-based methodologies is also very similar and in some or the other form always implies defining a comprehensive target architecture, comparing it with the existing IT landscape and then producing the implementation plan based on the identified gaps between the current and target architectures. All these methodologies advocate the same analysis-synthesis documentation-oriented plan-then-implement mechanistic attitude inspired by classic industrial engineering approaches, as if organizations can be planned and designed like buildings, ships or airplanes.

Due to their conceptual equivalency, the practical problems of all these architecture-based planning methodologies were always the same as well. These problems have been consistently reported from the mid-1980s to the present days by numerous independent researchers, observers and analysts [43, 44, 45, 46, 47, 48, 49, 50, 51, 52, 53, 54, 55, 56, 57, 58, 59, 60, 61, 62, 63, 64, 65]. All architecture-based planning methodologies required too much money, time and effort to execute. The resulting architectures were obsolete even before their completion. Moreover, these architectures were too technical, inflexible and unsuitable for decision-making. Architectural artifacts were considered as cryptic, arcane and inscrutable by their key stakeholders, especially by business leaders. Maintenance of these artifacts consumed enormous organizational resources. Architecture planning activities were disconnected from other organizational processes. The developed architectures were ignored by decision-makers and eventually turned into "shelfware" without being implemented or used in any real sense. The analysis of the historical evolution, meaning, attitude and problems of the stream of formal architecture-based planning methodologies described above is summarized in Figure 1.

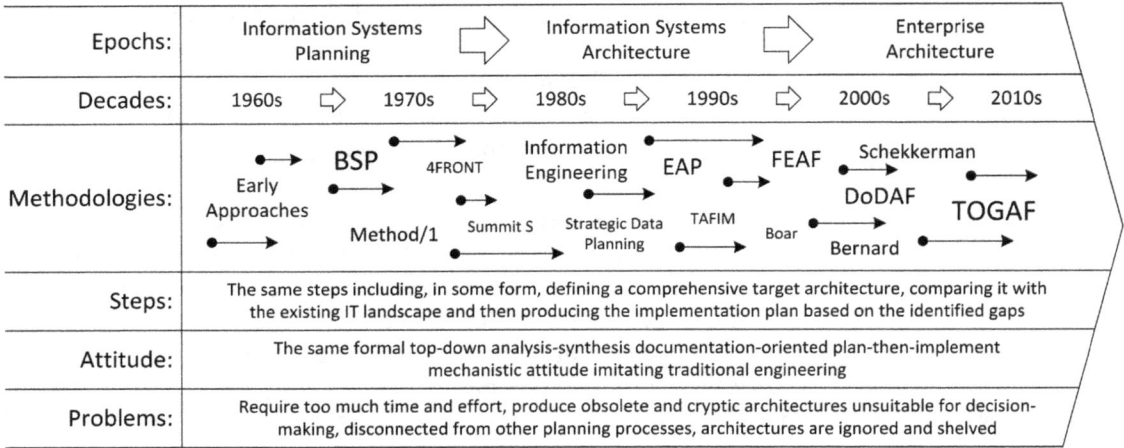

Epochs:	Information Systems Planning		Information Systems Architecture		Enterprise Architecture	
Decades:	1960s ⇨ 1970s	⇨	1980s ⇨ 1990s	⇨	2000s ⇨	2010s
Methodologies:	Early Approaches • → BSP • → 4FRONT • → Method/1 • →	Summit S • →	Information Engineering • → EAP • → Strategic Data Planning • → TAFIM • →	FEAF • → Boar • → Bernard • →	Schekkerman • → DoDAF • →	TOGAF • →
Steps:	The same steps including, in some form, defining a comprehensive target architecture, comparing it with the existing IT landscape and then producing the implementation plan based on the identified gaps					
Attitude:	The same formal top-down analysis-synthesis documentation-oriented plan-then-implement mechanistic attitude imitating traditional engineering					
Problems:	Require too much time and effort, produce obsolete and cryptic architectures unsuitable for decision-making, disconnected from other planning processes, architectures are ignored and shelved					

Figure 1. The stream of formal architecture-based planning methodologies

The historical analysis of the stream of formal architecture-based planning methodologies provided above clearly shows that all these methodologies represented only slightly different incarnations of the same pivotal planning approach and this approach always teemed with significant problems, never worked particularly well in organizations and demonstrated its practical ineffectiveness. Moreover, various independent researchers and observers at different time periods unanimously concluded that the problems with formal architecture-based planning methodologies, regardless of their current titles and "flavors", are fundamental in nature. For example, Goodhue et al. [45, p. 28] concluded that "the evidence [from nine organizations that used BSP and similar planning methodologies] presented here strongly supports the need for a fundamental rethinking of IS planning methodologies". Hamilton [63, p. 81] concluded that "findings from the study suggest strongly that the prescriptive approach to architecture-driven planning at the portfolio level is fundamentally flawed". Gaver [55, p. 10] concluded that "EA often doesn't work well anywhere because the problems with Enterprise Architecture [frameworks] are fundamental in nature". These conclusions suggest that *the entire stream of architecture-based planning methodologies is profoundly faulty in its essence*.

From the historical perspective, formal architecture-based planning methodologies can be considered only as typical management fads [66, 67, 68, 69], i.e. aggressively promoted management techniques of passing popularity and questionable efficacy. Historically, numerous architecture-based methodologies constantly emerged under different titles (see Figure 1). All these methodologies were actively promoted for certain time periods by their commercially motivated vendors, proved their impracticality, discredited themselves and faded away, but only to be replaced later with some "new" methodologies replicating the same old ideas under refreshing and innovative titles, often even promoted by the same vendors. Essentially, the entire stream of architecture-based planning methodologies can be considered as an evolving "breed" of mutating management fads continuously reproducing themselves, where older generations are periodically substituted with newer generations still having the same wicked "DNA".

Ironically, but acknowledged, well-documented, spectacular and extremely expensive failures of the latest generation of faddish and inherently flawed architecture-based methodologies, though again promoted as "proven best practices" by numerous irresponsible gurus and consultancies, can be openly found in the Internet. For example, the amazing practical "effectiveness" of FEAF can be vividly illustrated with the following quote from the report of a direct participant of the U.S. Federal Enterprise Architecture program: "Literally more than a billion dollars have been spent so far on Enterprise Architecture by the federal government, and much, if not most of it has been wasted" [55, p. 52]. Similarly, the "successes" of DoDAF can be illustrated with the following quote from the official audit report to the U.S. Congress: "Even though [the Department of Defense] has spent more than 10 years and at least $379 million on its business enterprise architecture, its ability to use the architecture to guide and constrain investments has been limited" [70, p. ii]. Historically, FEAF and DoDAF represent only the next attempts to "sell" the same flawed mechanistic planning approach pioneered by BSP and other early planning methods of the 1960s, and were doomed to fail from the very beginning of the corresponding U.S. government initiatives.

Even more ironically, exactly the same story had been also reported earlier specifically regarding TAFIM, the direct and "officially" acknowledged predecessor of TOGAF. Due to the well-known problems associated with all formal architecture-based planning methodologies listed earlier, TAFIM was retired as impractical: "TAFIM most certainly required a large investment of both time and money", "the elapsed time required to produce the architecture makes it close to obsolete before completion", "the end result is normally incomprehensible to a business-oriented audience and is harder to trace to the business strategy" and "due to some of these flaws, the TAFIM was abruptly cancelled" [71, p. 79]. Paradoxically, but now the very same ideas of TAFIM that previously proved impractical and contributed to its retirement are again embodied with only minor modifications in the current international "best seller" TOGAF.

The analysis of the historical situation with formal architecture-based planning methodologies and their latest generation, i.e. modern EA frameworks, clearly shows that the today's "proven Enterprise Architecture methodology and framework" TOGAF [1, p. 1] is nothing more than *a purest management fad based on the same plain old ideas that proved impractical long ago and never worked well in real organizations*. The step-wise planning methodology recommended by TOGAF ADM descends directly from the early information systems planning methodologies of the 1960s-1970s, while TOGAF itself is only the next offspring of the same "pedigree" of formal architecture-based planning methodologies. Historically, TOGAF "flows" in the same stream of architecture-based planning methodologies together with BSP, Method/1, Information Engineering, EAP, FEAF and all other earlier faddish methodologies (see Figure 1). From the evidence-based perspective, TOGAF is not a breakthrough, but merely a yet another flawed architecture-based planning methodology, just the next fad.

...That Turned into a New Religion

If the world was a perfectly logical place and people were completely free of cognitive biases, then TOGAF's story would be already over with a rather boring final. It would have been recognized as a management fad some time ago and peacefully forgotten like all the previous once-popular fads in the five-decades-old stream of architecture-based planning methodologies. For example, who now remembers the once-famous BSP methodology so actively promoted by IBM as "best practice" in information systems planning? Or, what about Information Engineering and its "fathers" Clive Finkelstein and James Martin who once enjoyed worldwide fame and recognition? These and many other analogous methodologies, e.g. Method/1, 4FRONT and EAP, had once been widely promoted, enriched their creators, proved impractical and disappeared without a trace. But if all the previous fads have gone, why TOGAF still did not?

Despite the endless problems with architecture-based planning methodologies, the promising potential of architecture itself, as some form of a systematic description of the relationship between business and IT, had been widely recognized by practitioners rather long ago [63, 72, 73]. Eventually certain genuine best practices in using architecture, and later enterprise architecture, *unrelated to flawed architecture-based methodologies* started to gradually emerge in industry, prove their practical effectiveness and then spread from organizations to organizations through hordes of "traveling" architects.

From the temporal perspective the propagation of these industry-born best practices seemingly coincided with the period of the most active TOGAF promotion. As a result, for many people the emergence of consistent industry-born best practices in using enterprise architecture became closely associated with TOGAF, even though any traceable cause-and-effect relationships between these best practices and TOGAF are missing. On the one hand, the actual prescriptions of TOGAF are impossible to implement successfully in practice, just like the prescriptions of all the previous discredited and forgotten methodologies from BSP to TAFIM. On the other hand, real EA best practices, e.g. using business capability models for focusing IT investments, among many others, are not described in TOGAF or any other architecture-based methodologies. In fact, the overlap between TOGAF and actual EA best practices is negligible and limited only to some trivial common-sense generalities, e.g. some EA artifacts are necessary for planning, all domains from business to infrastructure should be mutually aligned, both the current and desired states should be taken into account in some form, etc.

At the same time, The Open Group seemingly actively exploited the favorable but mistaken association between TOGAF and genuine EA best practices by attributing known EA success stories in organizations to the application of TOGAF, even when no actual relationship between them existed. For instance, The Open Group published on their website a long list of well-known organizations using TOGAF [74]. As part of my field studies I had a chance to visit five of these organizations and some of them indeed established rather successful and mature EA practices. However, these EA practices did not resemble the core TOGAF recommendations in any real sense. In particular, none of the five "officially" TOGAF-using organizations followed ADM steps or developed recommended EA artifacts [75, 76]. In every case the use of TOGAF was only declared, while practicing architects either considered it only as some general guidance without any specific far-reaching consequences, or in the most ironical cases did not even study its original text, but still knew that they used TOGAF. Essentially, *in all cases TOGAF proved to be only a superficial "signboard" under which very different approaches had been actually practiced.*

Another popular trick that was definitely widely used and is still actively exploited by countless TOGAF consultants and trainers is the proper "adaptation" of TOGAF. TOGAF salesmen usually admit that TOGAF cannot be understood literally and used directly, but rather needs to be properly adapted to the needs of organizations, though without explaining or clarifying how exactly this adaptation should be accomplished. Unsurprisingly, numerous elusive, obscure, meaningless and unconvincing descriptions of the practical use of TOGAF can be often found here and there, for example, the following one: "Organizations start with an open framework like the TOGAF framework, but as it gets customized and tailored, it adapts to an organization's culture to become their own "personalized" enterprise architecture model. As enterprise architecture matures in an organization, the TOGAF framework is still inside and powering their enterprise architecture but no longer very visible" [77, p. 16]. This deliberate mystification of the "adaptation" process can be considered as a natural and logical reaction of commercially motivated consultants on the abundant TOGAF criticism within the EA community. Essentially, the proclaimed need for unspecified but critically necessary "tailoring" provides the only possible way for TOGAF salesmen to elegantly explain the crying inconsistency between genuine EA best practices and deeply flawed recommendations of TOGAF.

Unfortunately, the situation with the incessant and irresponsible TOGAF promotion seemingly already went too far and confused too many people. Instead of rightfully acknowledging TOGAF as the next management fad in the 50-years-old stream of similar flawed architecture-based planning methodologies (see Figure 1) and discarding it as useless long time ago, the complex chain of peculiar historical circumstances described above has led essentially to the formation of a new religion called TOGAF, which rather rapidly disseminated across the EA community. Among the worshipers, TOGAF is praised as a collection of God-sent eternal EA best practices of non-empirical nature somehow defining the entire EA discipline, while the very existence of numerous earlier analogous methodologies that proved impractical is ignored or even denied.

The TOGAF faith is based on a number of simple quasi-religious beliefs that are usually taken for granted, even in the academic EA community, and cannot be proved or falsified with any evidence. These beliefs in some or the other form can be often heard in various TOGAF-related discussions and include, but are not limited to, the following deep-seated convictions:

- TOGAF provides a fundamental basis required for an EA practice
- TOGAF represents pure EA "theory", which should necessarily exist in any discipline and is always different from actual practice
- TOGAF cannot be implemented directly and must be tailored before use because every organization is different
- Although TOGAF may significantly differ from the resulting EA practice, it still provides the necessary starting point
- TOGAF is intrinsically helpful, provides a common language to architects and implicitly empowers EA practices

None of these beliefs can withstand a detailed scrutiny or a scientific critique. For instance, "providing fundamental basis" is no more than a general slogan that does not imply any specific actionable consequences. Theory can indeed deviate from practice, but theory is backed by sound evidence, while TOGAF contradicts all available evidence. Organizations indeed can be different, but key TOGAF prescriptions cannot be implemented in any of them regardless of their differences. Using TOGAF as a starting point can be clearly attributed to the fact that genuine EA best practices are not yet formally documented and EA practitioners often simply have nothing else to start from. Moreover, the vast majority of TOGAF-related beliefs contradict fundamental scientific principles, most importantly, so-called Occam's razor (explanations with the fewest assumptions should be preferred) and Russell's teapot (burden of proof lies upon a person making unfalsifiable claims).

However, instead of questioning the sales-driven TOGAF promotion campaign, many people willingly and uncritically accept the postulates of the TOGAF faith. Moreover, many TOGAF-converted people invent their own argumentation to protect TOGAF from criticism. For example, popular reasoning in TOGAF's favor includes, but is not limited to, the following common arguments:

- TOGAF is only a framework, it is not even intended to be implemented
- TOGAF is only a tool, it cannot be blamed for failures
- For an EA practice you need good people, TOGAF itself is not enough

Even though each of these arguments definitely contains a grain of truth, these arguments are still dangerous half-truths masking the real problem of TOGAF: *its recommendations are impractical and hardly overlap with genuine EA best practices even from the purely factual perspective*, e.g. what activities should be carried out and what EA artifacts should be developed to improve business and IT alignment.

The ongoing confusion around TOGAF is seemingly also further aggravated by numerous direct inconsistencies and overall vagueness of the original TOGAF text. As Wierda [78, p. 67] fairly notices, "it is rather ironic that enterprise architecture frameworks [meaning TOGAF], their followers generally preaching a "fundamentals" or "highlevel" approach to design, consist of hundreds of pages of often inconsistent detail". Essentially, TOGAF can be interpreted in multiple different ways and for many people represents only a "dictionary" where some EA-related terms can be found, but a meaningful end-to-end story is missing altogether. This inherent ambiguity of TOGAF spawns diverse and often curious interpretations of its true "hidden" meaning. For instance, one of the most recent and definitely the most paradoxical interpretation suggests that TOGAF is actually a solution architecture framework.

Finally, the extreme popularity, "success" and semi-religious admiration of specifically TOGAF (rather than any other architecture-based planning methodology) arguably can be considered as a purely accidental phenomenon. From the historical perspective, TOGAF is not new and not conceptually different from numerous previous architecture-based methodologies starting from BSP introduced in the end of the 1960s. The elevation of TOGAF out of the broad stream of multiple highly similar methodologies (see Figure 1) can be seemingly attributed to its comprehensive volume, intensive promotion and, most importantly, to its very lucky timing. In particular, TOGAF was promoted specifically during the time period when authentic industry-born EA best practices unrelated to TOGAF started to emerge and actively spread across the industry, the critical factor that was missing for all the previous prominent planning methodologies, e.g. BSP and Information Engineering. If these genuine best practices emerged earlier during the 1980s, when Information Engineering was at the very peak of its promotional intensity, then Information Engineering might have become the same type of religion instead of TOGAF. Likewise, if these best practices started to emerge only later, say, during the 2020s, then some hypothetical next faddish architecture-based methodology, e.g. BOGAF, DOGAF or ZOGAF, might have become a religion. However, since these best practices actually emerged exactly during the period of the aggressive TOGAF promotion, specifically TOGAF was the next faddish architecture-based planning methodology that turned into a new religion.

Conclusion

The curious story briefly outlined above describes how just the next management fad, which does not even deserve any special attention due to its obviousness, through aggressive marketing, irresponsible promotion, deceptive tricks and pure coincidence essentially turned into a new religion. While numerous earlier architecture-based planning methodologies proved impractical and naturally became history, TOGAF advocating exactly the same flawed and long-discredited ideas that cannot work successfully in practice suddenly became reality for many people. At the same time, the evident inconsistency between TOGAF and genuine EA best practices is tolerated, the practical problems of TOGAF are ignored and their discussion is substituted with vague and misguiding explanations ranging from commonplace ones, e.g. TOGAF needs to be applied wisely, to rather exotic ones, e.g. TOGAF is actually intended for solution architecture.

The curious story of TOGAF can be considered as a brilliant victory of marketing and, at the same time, as a shameful loss of evidence-based research and common sense in general. On the one hand, TOGAF promoters were able to persuade numerous educated people that "black is white", i.e. sell proven worst practices essentially as new best practices even without demonstrating any examples of their successful practical implementation. On the other hand, due to the passive and overly "theoretical" attitude the academic EA community, with some notable exceptions, was generally unable to spot the faddish nature of TOGAF and effectively communicate the realistic information to the practitioner community, let alone propose a better evidence-based alternative to flawed architecture-based planning methodologies. This fact is especially disappointing since the acute problems with early architecture-based methodologies had been studied and reported long ago in the most prestigious academic journal MIS Quarterly [45, 46, 49], but subsequently these findings were ignored and forgotten even by the academics themselves.

The semi-religious nature of TOGAF generally has a very negative impact on the entire EA discipline. Like any religion, the TOGAF faith is based on certain dogmas, rather than on established facts, and the persistent focus on the same permanent dogmas essentially blocks the real progress and normal development of the EA discipline. Endless elusive TOGAF-centered discussions, e.g. how to use TOGAF properly or adapt it to the organizational culture, only distract the attention of the EA community from the actual problems, while evidence-based attempts to analyze genuine EA best practices still remain rather limited [78, 79, 80, 81, 82, 83, 84, 85].

Unfortunately, the TOGAF faith arguably came here to stay and is unlikely to go away in the near future. Therefore, members of the EA community should be prepared to adequately react on it and resist the aggressive TOGAF propaganda. In particular, EA practitioners should clearly understand the impracticality of TOGAF, trust their own common sense and "gut feeling" and switch their attention on learning, sharing and exchanging genuine EA best practices that proved effective in real organizations, while EA academics should finally acknowledge the faddish nature of TOGAF and start studying EA practices in a TOGAF-free manner.

References

[1] The Open Group (2016) "TOGAF Worldwide", The Open Group, URL: http://www.opengroup.org/subjectareas/enterprise/togaf/worldwide.

[2] Evans, M. K. and Hague, L. R. (1962) "Master Plan for Information Systems", *Harvard Business Review*, Vol. 40, No. 1, pp. 92-103.

[3] Schwartz, M. H. (1970) "MIS Planning", *Datamation*, Vol. 16, No. 10, pp. 28-31.

[4] BSP (1975) "Business Systems Planning: Information Systems Planning Guide (1st Edition)" (#GE20-0527-1), White Plains, NY: IBM Corporation.

[5] Orsey, R. R. (1982) "Business Systems Planning: Management of Information", *Computer Decisions*, Vol. 14, No. 2, pp. 154-158.

[6] Vacca, J. R. (1983) "BSP: How Is It Working?", *Computerworld*, Vol. 17, No. 12, pp. 9-18.

[7] Kotusev, S. (2016) "The History of Enterprise Architecture: An Evidence-Based Review", *Journal of Enterprise Architecture*, Vol. 12, No. 1, pp. 29-37.

[8] Remenyi, D. (1991) *Introducing Strategic Information Systems Planning*, Manchester, UK: NCC Blackwell.

[9] Nolan, R. L. and Mulryan, D. W. (1987) "Undertaking an Architecture Program", *Stage by Stage*, Vol. 7, No. 2, pp. 1-10.

[10] Arthur Andersen (1979) "Method/1: Systems Development Practices", Chicago, IL: Arthur Andersen.

[11] Gallo, T. E. (1988) *Strategic Information Management Planning*, Englewood Cliffs, NJ: Prentice Hall.

[12] Inmon, W. H. (1986) *Information Systems Architecture: A System Developer's Primer*, Englewood Cliffs, NJ: Prentice Hall.

[13] Tozer, E. E. (1988) *Planning for Effective Business Information Systems*, Oxford, UK: Pergamon Press.

[14] TAFIM (1996) "Department of Defense Technical Architecture Framework for Information Management, Volume 4: DoD Standards-Based Architecture Planning Guide (Version 3.0)", Arlington County, VA: Defense Information Systems Agency.

[15] GAO (1992) "Strategic Information Planning: Framework for Designing and Developing System Architectures" (#GAO/IMTEC-92-51), Washington, DC: Government Accountability Office.

[16] BSP (1984) "Business Systems Planning: Information Systems Planning Guide (4th Edition)" (#GE20-0527-4), Atlanta, GA: IBM Corporation.

[17] Finkelstein, C. (1981) "Information Engineering (Reprint of Computerworld Issues Dated May 11, May 25, June 1, June 8 and June 15 of 1981)", Englewood Cliffs, NJ: Prentice Hall.

[18] Martin, J. and Finkelstein, C. (1981) *Information Engineering (Volumes I and II)*, Carnforth, The United Kingdom: Savant Institute.

[19] Inmon, W. H. (1988) *Information Engineering for the Practitioner: Putting Theory into Practice*, Englewood Cliffs, NJ: Yourdon Press.

[20] Arthur Young (1987) *The Arthur Young Practical Guide to Information Engineering*, New York, NY: Wiley.

[21] Finkelstein, C. (1989) *An Introduction to Information Engineering: From Strategic Planning to Information Systems*, Sydney, Australia: Addison-Wesley.

[22] Martin, J. (1989) *Information Engineering (Book I: Introduction, Book II: Planning and Analysis, Book III: Design and Construction)*, Englewood Cliffs, NJ: Prentice Hall.

[23] Martin, J. (1982) *Strategic Data-Planning Methodologies*, Englewood Cliffs, NJ: Prentice Hall.

[24] Martin, J. and Leben, J. (1989) *Strategic Information Planning Methodologies (2nd Edition)*, Englewood Cliffs, NJ: Prentice Hall.

[25] Spewak, S. H. and Hill, S. C. (1992) *Enterprise Architecture Planning: Developing a Blueprint for Data, Applications and Technology*, New York, NY: Wiley.

[26] FEAF (1999) "Federal Enterprise Architecture Framework, Version 1.1", Springfield, VA: Chief Information Officer Council.

[27] Boar, B. H. (1999) *Constructing Blueprints for Enterprise IT Architectures*, New York, NY: Wiley.

[28] Schekkerman, J. (2008) *Enterprise Architecture Good Practices Guide: How to Manage the Enterprise Architecture Practice*, Victoria, BC: Trafford Publishing.

[29] Bernard, S. A. (2004) *An Introduction to Enterprise Architecture (1st Edition)*, Bloomington, IN: AuthorHouse.

[30] DoDAF (2007) "The DoDAF Architecture Framework, Version 1.5 (Volume I: Definitions and Guidelines)", Arlington County, VA: Department of Defense.

[31] Cook, M. A. (1996) *Building Enterprise Information Architectures: Reengineering Information Systems*, Upper Saddle River, NJ: Prentice Hall.

[32] Armour, F. J., Kaisler, S. H. and Liu, S. Y. (1999) "Building an Enterprise Architecture Step by Step", *IT Professional*, Vol. 1, No. 4, pp. 31-39.

[33] Bittler, R. S. and Kreizman, G. (2005) "Gartner Enterprise Architecture Process: Evolution 2005" (#G00130849), Stamford, CT: Gartner.

[34] Covington, R. and Jahangir, H. (2009) "The Oracle Enterprise Architecture Framework", Redwood Shores, CA: Oracle.

[35] Theuerkorn, F. (2004) *Lightweight Enterprise Architectures*, Boca Raton, FL: Auerbach Publications.

[36] van't Wout, J., Waage, M., Hartman, H., Stahlecker, M. and Hofman, A. (2010) *The Integrated Architecture Framework Explained: Why, What, How*, Berlin: Springer.

[37] Niemann, K. D. (2006) *From Enterprise Architecture to IT Governance: Elements of Effective IT Management*, Wiesbaden: Vieweg.

[38] Longepe, C. (2003) *The Enterprise Architecture IT Project: The Urbanisation Paradigm*, London: Kogan Page Science.

[39] IBM (2006) "An Introduction to IBM's Enterprise Architecture Consulting Method", Armonk, NY: IBM Global Services.

[40] Carbone, J. A. (2004) *IT Architecture Toolkit*, Upper Saddle River, NJ: Prentice Hall.

[41] Holcman, S. B. (2013) *Reaching the Pinnacle: A Methodology of Business Understanding, Technology Planning, and Change*, Pinckney, MI: Pinnacle Business Group Inc.

[42] TOGAF (2011) "TOGAF Version 9.1" (#G116), The Open Group.

[43] Lohe, J. and Legner, C. (2014) "Overcoming Implementation Challenges in Enterprise Architecture Management: A Design Theory for Architecture-Driven IT Management (ADRIMA)", *Information Systems and e-Business Management*, Vol. 12, No. 1, pp. 101-137.

[44] Kim, Y.-G. and Everest, G. C. (1994) "Building an IS Architecture: Collective Wisdom from the Field", *Information and Management*, Vol. 26, No. 1, pp. 1-11.

[45] Goodhue, D. L., Kirsch, L. J., Quillard, J. A. and Wybo, M. D. (1992) "Strategic Data Planning: Lessons from the Field", *MIS Quarterly*, Vol. 16, No. 1, pp. 11-34.

[46] Goodhue, D. L., Quillard, J. A. and Rockart, J. F. (1988) "Managing the Data Resource: A Contingency Perspective", *MIS Quarterly*, Vol. 12, No. 3, pp. 373-392.

[47] Shanks, G. (1997) "The Challenges of Strategic Data Planning in Practice: An Interpretive Case Study", *Journal of Strategic Information Systems*, Vol. 6, No. 1, pp. 69-90.

[48] Lederer, A. L. and Sethi, V. (1992) "Meeting the Challenges of Information Systems Planning", *Long Range Planning*, Vol. 25, No. 2, pp. 69-80.

[49] Lederer, A. L. and Sethi, V. (1988) "The Implementation of Strategic Information Systems Planning Methodologies", *MIS Quarterly*, Vol. 12, No. 3, pp. 445-461.

[50] Kemp, P. and McManus, J. (2009) "Whither Enterprise Architecture?", *ITNOW Computing Journal*, Vol. 51, No. 2, pp. 20-21.

[51] Bloomberg, J. (2014) "Is Enterprise Architecture Completely Broken?", Forbes, URL: http://www.forbes.com/sites/jasonbloomberg/2014/07/11/is-enterprise-architecture-completely-broken/.

[52] Holst, M. S. and Steensen, T. W. (2011) "The Successful Enterprise Architecture Effort", *Journal of Enterprise Architecture*, Vol. 7, No. 4, pp. 16-22.

[53] Beynon-Davies, P. (1994) "Information Management in the British National Health Service: The Pragmatics of Strategic Data Planning", *International Journal of Information Management*, Vol. 14, No. 2, pp. 84-94.

[54] Trionfi, A. (2016) "Guiding Principles to Support Organization-Level Enterprise Architectures", *Journal of Enterprise Architecture*, Vol. 12, No. 3, pp. 40-45.

[55] Gaver, S. B. (2010) "Why Doesn't the Federal Enterprise Architecture Work?", McLean, VA: Technology Matters.

[56] GAO (2015) "DOD Business Systems Modernization: Additional Action Needed to Achieve Intended Outcomes" (#GAO-15-627), Washington, DC: Government Accountability Office.

[57] Goodhue, D. L., Quillard, J. A. and Rockart, J. F. (1986) "The Management of Data: Preliminary Research Results", Cambridge, MA: Center for Information Systems Research (CISR), MIT Sloan School of Management.

[58] Shanks, G. and Swatman, P. (1997) "Building and Using Corporate Data Models: A Case Study of Four Australian Banks", In: Gable, G. and Weber, R. (eds.) *Proceedings of the 3rd Pacific Asia Conference on Information Systems*, Brisbane, Australia: Association for Information Systems, pp. 815-825.

[59] Davenport, T. H. (1994) "Saving IT's Soul: Human-Centered Information Management", *Harvard Business Review*, Vol. 72, No. 2, pp. 119-131.

[60] Kotusev, S. (2016) "Enterprise Architecture Frameworks: The Fad of the Century", British Computer Society (BCS), URL: http://www.bcs.org/content/conWebDoc/56347.

[61] Tucci, L. (2011) "Two IT Gurus Face Off on Value of Enterprise Architecture Frameworks", TotalCIO, URL: http://itknowledgeexchange.techtarget.com/total-cio/two-it-gurus-face-off-on-value-of-enterprise-architecture-frameworks/.

[62] Seppanen, V., Heikkila, J. and Liimatainen, K. (2009) "Key Issues in EA-Implementation: Case Study of Two Finnish Government Agencies", In: Hofreiter, B. and Werthner, H. (eds.) *Proceedings of the 11th IEEE Conference on Commerce and Enterprise Computing*, Vienna: IEEE, pp. 114-120.

[63] Hamilton, D. (1999) "Linking Strategic Information Systems Concepts to Practice: Systems Integration at the Portfolio Level", *Journal of Information Technology*, Vol. 14, No. 1, pp. 69-82.

[64] Legner, C. and Lohe, J. (2012) "Embedding EAM into Operation and Monitoring", In: Ahlemann, F., Stettiner, E., Messerschmidt, M. and Legner, C. (eds.) *Strategic Enterprise Architecture Management: Challenges, Best Practices, and Future Developments*, Berlin: Springer, pp. 169-199.

[65] Segars, A. H. and Grover, V. (1996) "Designing Company-Wide Information Systems: Risk Factors and Coping Strategies", *Long Range Planning*, Vol. 29, No. 3, pp. 381-392.

[66] Miller, D. and Hartwick, J. (2002) "Spotting Management Fads", *Harvard Business Review*, Vol. 80, No. 10, pp. 26-27.

[67] Miller, D., Hartwick, J. and Le Breton-Miller, I. (2004) "How to Detect a Management Fad - And Distinguish It From a Classic", *Business Horizons*, Vol. 47, No. 4, pp. 7-16.

[68] Abrahamson, E. (1991) "Managerial Fads and Fashions: The Diffusion and Rejection of Innovations", *Academy of Management Review*, Vol. 16, No. 3, pp. 586-612.

[69] Abrahamson, E. (1996) "Management Fashion", *Academy of Management Review*, Vol. 21, No. 1, pp. 254-285.

[70] GAO (2013) "DOD Business Systems Modernization: Further Actions Needed to Address Challenges and Improve Accountability" (#GAO-13-557), Washington, DC: Government Accountability Office.

[71] Perks, C. and Beveridge, T. (2003) *Guide to Enterprise IT Architecture*, New York, NY: Springer.

[72] Periasamy, K. P. (1993) "The State and Status of Information Architecture: An Empirical Investigation", In: DeGross, J. I., Bostrom, R. P. and Robey, D. (eds.) *Proceedings of the 14th International Conference on Information Systems*, Orlando, FL: Association for Information Systems, pp. 255-270.

[73] Periasamy, K. P. and Feeny, D. F. (1997) "Information Architecture Practice: Research-Based Recommendations for the Practitioner", *Journal of Information Technology*, Vol. 12, No. 3, pp. 197-205.

[74] The Open Group (2016) "TOGAF Users by Market Sector", The Open Group, URL: http://web.archive.org/web/20151121161238/http://www.opengroup.org/togaf/users-by-market-sector.

[75] Kotusev, S. (2016) "Enterprise Architecture Is Not TOGAF", British Computer Society (BCS), URL: http://www.bcs.org/content/conWebDoc/55547.

[76] Kotusev, S. (2016) "The Critical Scrutiny of TOGAF", British Computer Society (BCS), URL: http://www.bcs.org/content/conWebDoc/55892.

[77] Viswanathan, V. (2015) "Four Questions: Vish Viswanathan", *Journal of Enterprise Architecture*, Vol. 11, No. 2, pp. 15-17.

[78] Wierda, G. (2015) *Chess and the Art of Enterprise Architecture*, Amsterdam: R&A.

[79] Kotusev, S. (2016) "Six Types of Enterprise Architecture Artifacts", British Computer Society (BCS), URL: http://www.bcs.org/content/conWebDoc/57097.

[80] Kotusev, S. (2017) "Eight Essential Enterprise Architecture Artifacts", British Computer Society (BCS), URL: http://www.bcs.org/content/conWebDoc/57318.

[81] Kotusev, S. (2017) "The Relationship Between Enterprise Architecture Artifacts", British Computer Society (BCS), URL: http://www.bcs.org/content/conWebDoc/57563.

[82] Kotusev, S. (2017) "Enterprise Architecture on a Single Page", British Computer Society (BCS), URL: http://www.bcs.org/content/conWebDoc/58615.

[83] Ross, J. W., Weill, P. and Robertson, D. C. (2006) *Enterprise Architecture as Strategy: Creating a Foundation for Business Execution*, Boston, MA: Harvard Business School Press.

[84] Murer, S., Bonati, B. and Furrer, F. J. (2011) *Managed Evolution: A Strategy for Very Large Information Systems*, Berlin: Springer.

[85] Ahlemann, F., Stettiner, E., Messerschmidt, M. and Legner, C. (eds.) (2012) *Strategic Enterprise Architecture Management: Challenges, Best Practices, and Future Developments*, Berlin: Springer.

TOM GRAVES - TETRADIAN

How do I loathe thee, TOGAF®? Let me count the ways…

By Tom Graves (Tetradian)

4 November 2014

In case anyone thinks that I'm just 'TOGAF-bashing' for the sake of it, I *do* believe that TOGAF has genuine value *for what it was originally designed to do*, namely architecture of enterprise-wide IT-infrastructure.

TOGAF 8.1 was actually pretty good at that, though by 2009 it was an urgent need of an update. Yet as I wrote back in February 2009, after the TOGAF 9 launch, to me **TOGAF 9 represented a huge missed-opportunity, a disastrous hubris-laden wrong-turn**. There were two choices: either stay with IT-architecture, and really develop the meta-architectures so as to make it self-updating to each change in technology (which was well within Open Group's capabilities and remit); or go all-out to support a true 'architecture of the enterprise' (which, as an *IT-standards* body, Open Group was perhaps not well placed to do). In the end, they chose the worst of both worlds: a vaguely-revamped static framework that couldn't keep pace with technological change, and that retained the inherently IT-centric 'BDAT-stack' yet also pretended that it would still work beyond IT (which, *by definition*, it can't).

To be blunt, the current version of TOGAF looks like, and is, a classic example of a framework cobbled together out of disparate parts by a 200+ person committee. There are some excellent bits in it – my favourite is probably Bob Weisman's work on capability-architectures – but overall it's best described as a bloated, hugely-oversized, often-misleading, largely unusable mess. Even the ADM is a badly-reworked PDCA loop, with a misleadingly-constrained 'Act' phase (ADM Phases B/C/D) and virtually no 'Check' phase (no 'benefits-realisation' or 'lessons-learned' in ADM Phases H/A).

Whilst TOGAF 8.1 was an IT-architecture framework that was good at what it did but needed some updating, TOGAF 9 and 9.1 are less-complete IT-architecture frameworks that are desperately pretending to be more than they are, and in practice are just-about usable only for the kind of now quite old big-IT that's still in use only a specific subset of industries such as banking, insurance, finance and tax. There's almost nothing in there that will help much, if at all, with mobile or social or internet-of-things or embedded health-technologies or 'human apps' such as Amazon's 'Mechanical Turk', or even key aspects of IT-disaster-recovery, because those are all contexts in which the human is deeply interwoven with the physical-machine is deeply-interwoven with the IT-technical is deeply interwoven with enterprise-purpose – whereas TOGAF and Archimate and the like *only* tackle the IT, leaving everything else as a supposedly all-but-irrelevant afterthought, a Somebody Else's Problem.

The catch is that, as enterprise-architects, we *are* that 'Somebody Else': it's *our* Problem. And we *need* real usable tools and frameworks to help us with that problem. Yet despite its vaunted claims to the contrary, TOGAF 9.1 is most definitely not one of them: it's unsuited for the purpose, right down to the deepest roots of its internal architecture. But because it sits there like a dog-in-the-manger, hogging almost the entirety of that space, we're stuck: none of us can move forward until we have some means to fix the resultant TOGAF-driven IT-centric mess.

Sigh…

To illustrate the point, let's start with the centrepiece for TOGAF, the ADM (Architecture Development Method), and play a quick game of 'Spot The Difference'. Before we do that, let's first have a quick check of the criteria for a framework that could actually work at a true whole-of-enterprise scope:

- It needs to be able to cover *any* scope and context, consistent yet self-adapting to all those different contexts.
- It needs to be able to work on any subsets of the overall scope, whilst still retaining full connection to that overall scope.
- It needs to be able to work with and develop for often-extreme uncertainty.
- It needs to support the full range from big-picture to detail-level, and from vision and strategy to implementation and operation.
- It needs to support continuous-learning and continuous improvement.
- In a business-sense, it needs to support real business-value.

Given that list, let's play Spot The Difference on the TOGAF ADM, versus an alternate methodology that follows what, on the surface, might seem to be the same structure:

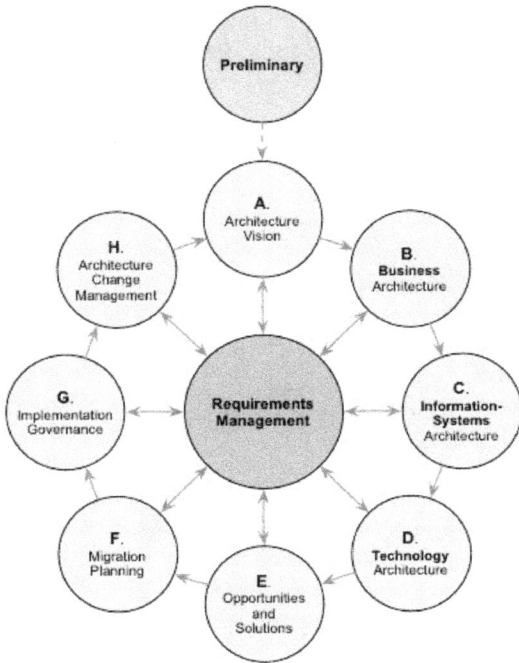

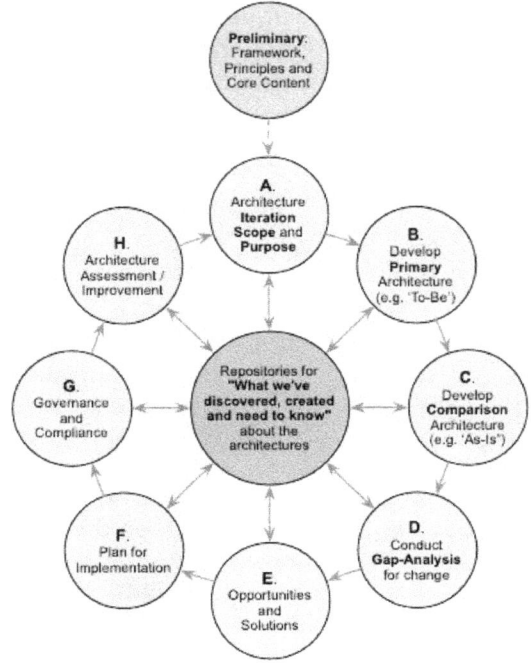

No doubt you've noticed all of the differences. But have you noticed *why* the differences exist, and what they imply in practice?

The graphic on the left side of that 'Spot The Difference' summarises a *method* — the standard TOGAF9 ADM. And *as* a method, it's optimised for use in precisely *one* type of context — a specific form of IT-architecture — and in practice is too constrained to do almost anything else:

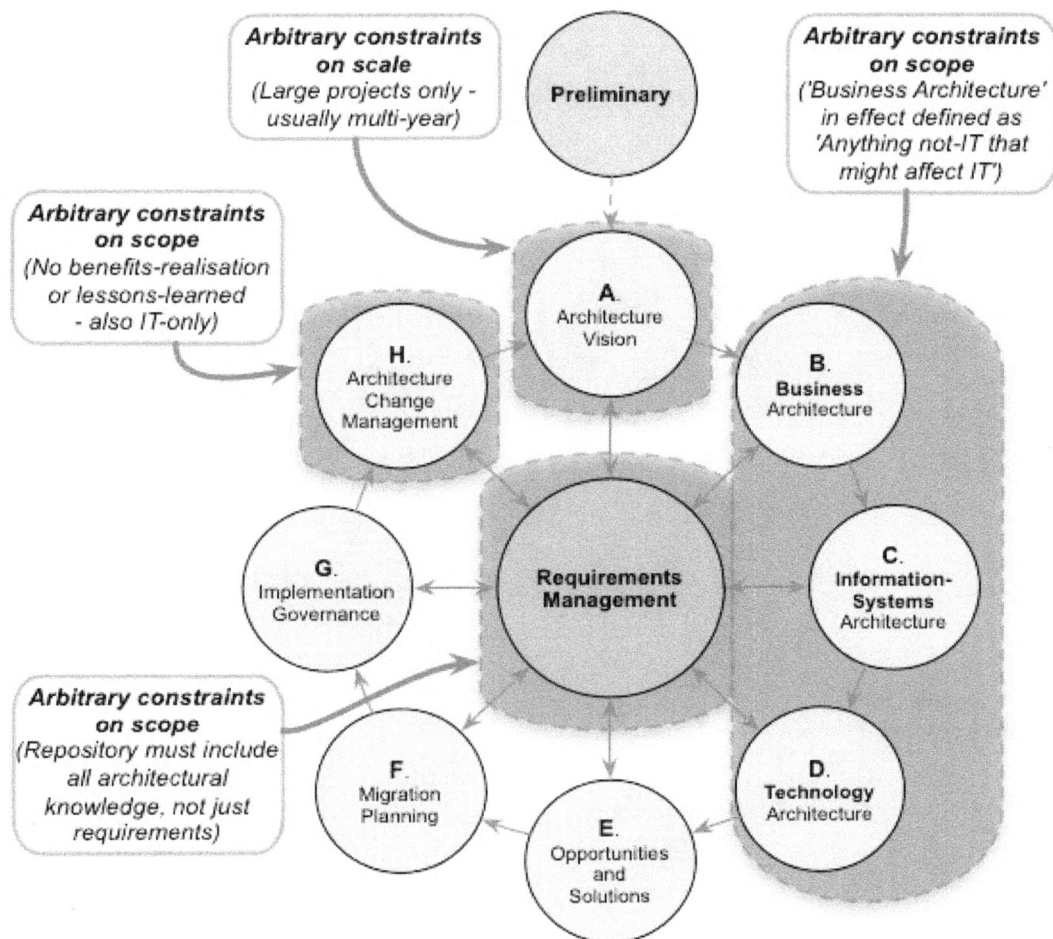

Arbitrary constraints on scale
(Large projects only - usually multi-year)

Preliminary

Arbitrary constraints on scope
('Business Architecture' in effect defined as 'Anything not-IT that might affect IT')

Arbitrary constraints on scope
(No benefits-realisation or lessons-learned - also IT-only)

H. Architecture Change Management

A. Architecture Vision

B. Business Architecture

G. Implementation Governance

Requirements Management

C. Information-Systems Architecture

Arbitrary constraints on scope
(Repository must include all architectural knowledge, not just requirements)

F. Migration Planning

E. Opportunities and Solutions

D. Technology Architecture

Implicit from the arrows on the graphic is that it is *possible* to use it in a non-linear way – though this is barely described in the documentation, with no actual instructions on how to *do* it.

The graphic on the right side of that 'Spot The Difference' summarises a *metamethod*. And *as* a metamethod, it can be used either as-is, or in a *self-adapting* way to create *context-specific* methods for *any* type of scope and context – including (if with some twists) the TOGAF ADM itself:

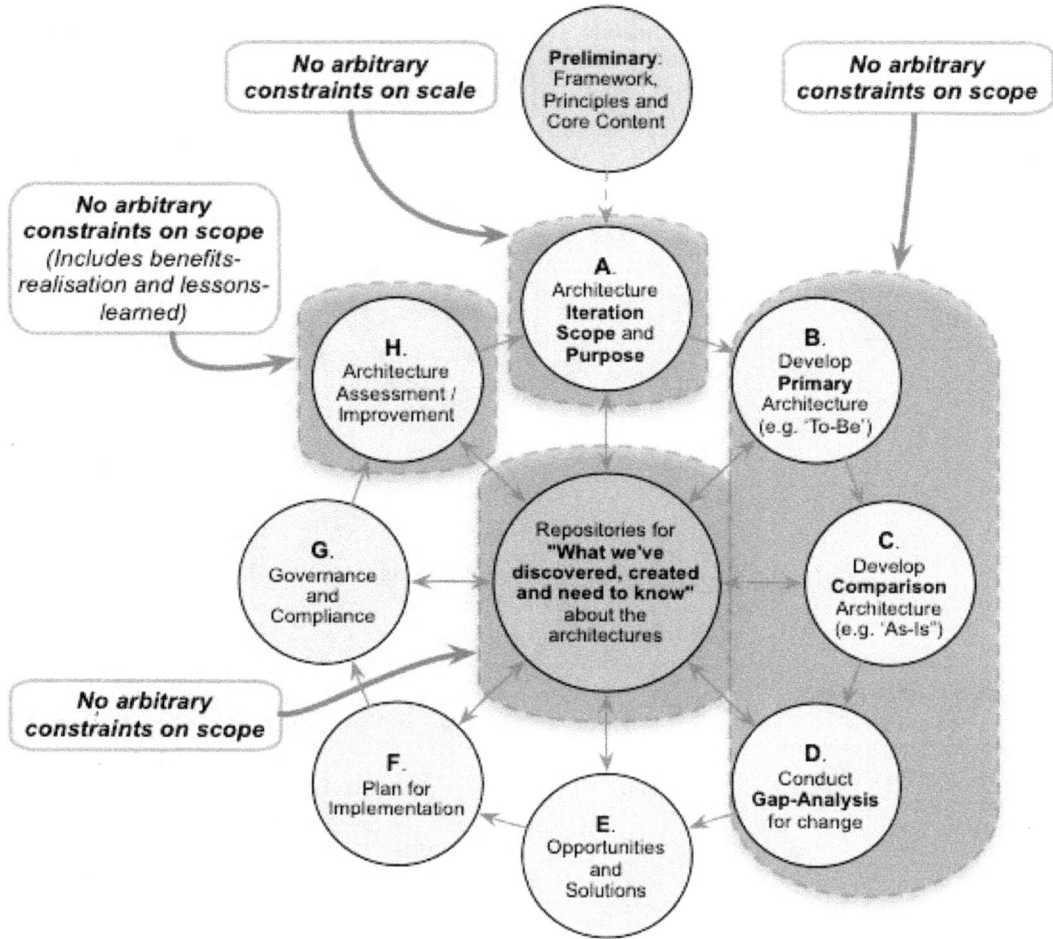

(Note that it's not that there's no scope in Phases B, C and D, or that the scope is always an impossible 'The Everything' – but rather than the respective scope for the iteration is identified and defined in Phase A. That means that we can work on *any* scope, including subsets, supersets or intersecting-sets of the current scope, recursively, yet still do so in way that is clearly identifiable and appropriately-constrained *for the current iteration*.)

Implicit from the arrows on the graphic is that it can likewise be used in a non-linear way – but also fully-recursive, via the 'any scope, any scale' structure of Phases A to D.

(To be pedantic, that graphic on the right is itself an instance of a *metametamethod* for continuous-change and continuous-improvement. of which, for example, PDCA, OODA and the classic Tuckman 'Group Dynamics' project-cycle are other instances.)

Nothing much wrong with having a method like that of the ADM, that only works well with one type of scope and context, of course – *as long as that scope and context are all it'd be used for*.

The catch is that, courtesy of the hype-machine that is behind TOGAF these days, **the graphic on the left is insistently marketed and 'sold' as if it's the graphic on the right** – as if the tiny subset of scope that the TOGAF ADM *can* cover is all that anyone would ever need in enterprise-architecture. Which it isn't.

Which, since TOGAF *can't* actually handle anything more than a very narrow type of scope – because that scope is *hardwired* right into its very structure – makes life very difficult indeed for those of us who *do* work at wider scopes and the rest of that list of criteria near the start of this post, and have to spend inordinate effort tidying up the TOGAF-created mess.

Bah.

But as enterprise-architects, that's just the *start* of our TOGAF-created woes... Here are a few more:

Pseudo-'non-proprietary' versus real non-proprietary

Proprietary frameworks are bad news all round: that's all that need be said on that.

Open Group do claim that TOGAF is 'non-proprietary'. Yet I'd put quotes around that assertion, because calling TOGAF a 'non-proprietary framework' really *is* a stretch too far: it may be true that we might not have to pay to, uh, look at it, but that's about it. 'Freemium', just possibly: but the kind of 'freemium' that we can't act *do* anything useful with unless we pony-up on the in-app purchases…

That's because TOGAF itself is too incomplete to use 'as-is': there are key chunks missing, which means that it is, in effect, misleadingly useless, giving the *impression* of usability without actually providing it – kind of like a car that looks all shiny and new and ready to go but with key less-visible components like the drive-shaft and the steering-rods somehow just not there. In fact on its own, 'out of the box', the only people who *could* use TOGAF are those who already know enough real-world EA to be able to do without it – so the whole thing is all a bit moot anyway.

To make this 'standard' 'non-proprietary' framework usable in real-world practice, there's a sizeable training-industry, all of it licensed at a fee to Open Group, and at serious cost to participants: back-of-the-envelope calculation suggests mid- to high tens of millions of dollars so far, and rising. And then there's the 'certification': tested by multiple-choice exam – exactly how *not* to do skills-evaluation – and again a 'nice little earner', currently in the low tens of millions of dollars. 'Non-proprietary'? Marketing hype-machine, yes, but 'non-proprietary' in any real sense of the word? – I think not…

True non-proprietary frameworks for EA do indeed exist: Kevin Smith's PEAF and POET pairing is one that comes immediately to mind. Milan Guenther's book '*Intersection*', on enterprise design, and Marlies Steenbergen and Martin Van Den Berg's '*Building An Enterprise Architecture Practice*', on the DyA framework, are a lot more complete and usable than TOGAF, and also both come close to true non-proprietary, too: to get the full detail you'd have to buy the book, but that's all.

To me the ideal would be some form of open-source architecture-framework – but it still doesn't seem to be happening in any workable form as yet. Oh well.

Enterprise-as-scope versus enterprise-as-domain

This is probably the single most misleading mistake in the whole of TOGAF, yet in some ways one of the hardest to see: conflating 'enterprise' as a *scope*, with 'enterprise' as a *domain* in its own right.

In its Introduction, the TOGAF specification does define 'enterprise' in several ways: an organisation, a consortium of organisations, and so on. But what it *doesn't* do is say – anywhere, as far as I can tell – that this is merely the *scope* of interest, to which all of the following specification would apply. It's IT-architecture at an enterprise-wide scale, yes – *but that's not the same as 'enterprise-architecture'*, the literal 'architecture of the enterprise', where the enterprise *itself* is the domain of interest.

As described in the post 'Organisation and enterprise', the scope we *actually* need to explore – the respective 'enterprise' – for any given architecture is at least two to three steps larger than the main scope of interest. At a whole-of-organisation level, for example, the respective 'enterprise' that we'd need to explore stretches way out beyond even the organisation's business-market:

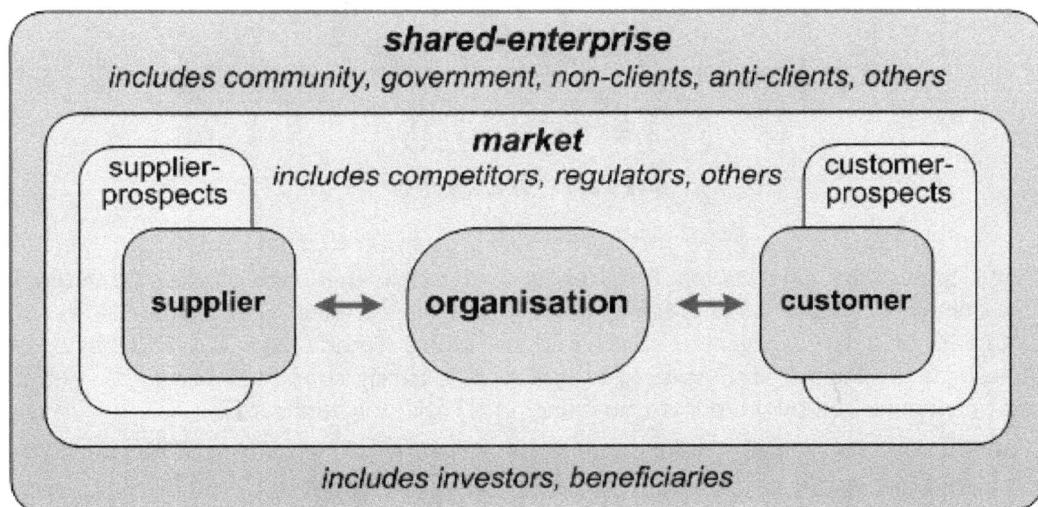

Yet TOGAF strongly implies, throughout the specification, that the organisation *itself* is 'the enterprise', the ultimate boundary of any architecture. As described in that 'Organisation and enterprise' post, this has *serious* consequences if we try to apply it at a business-architecture level, and often below that level as well.

That one double-error of conflation – perpetrated and perpetuated throughout the entire specification – leaves the framework wide-open to risk of perpetrating *really* serious term-hijacks, in which a tiny subset of a scope pretends to be the whole, blocking out the view of anything other than itself. Which is precisely what we see next, with the bewretched 'BDAT-stack'…

BDAT-stack versus real-world

Like Archimate, which in essence follows the same pattern, TOGAF purports that the entirety of an enterprise-architecture can be split into exactly three sub-architectures:

- Business Architecture
- Information-Systems Architecture
- Technology Architecture

In TOGAF itself, Information-Systems Architecture may optionally be split into Data-Architecture and Applications-Architecture – hence the respective initials that give us that acronym 'BDAT', 'Business, Data, Applications, Technology'.

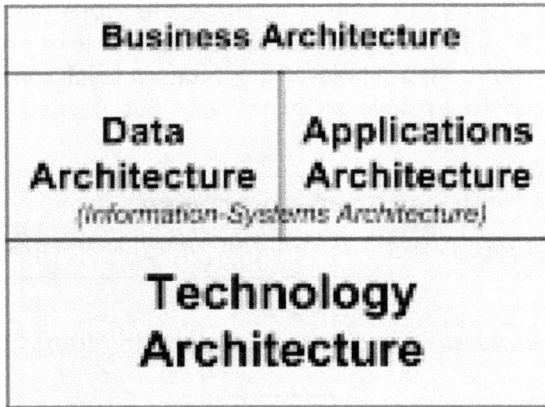

Looking closer at the specification, it quickly becomes clear that each of these 'architectures' revolves entirely around what we might call 'big-IT' – the kind of systems run by an 'IT Department' of a large organisation of perhaps half a decade ago. It's *really* obvious, for example, that the supposed 'Business Architecture' is barely about business at all, but could instead be summarised by the phrase 'anything not-IT that might affect IT'.

The BDAT-stack is actually quite a good description of what's needed for a big-IT infrastructure-architecture, where – in terms of that 'enterprise' model just above – 'Information-Systems Architecture' is the metaphoric equivalent of 'suppliers and customers', and 'Business Architecture' is the metaphoric equivalent of the 'market'-space for that big-IT. But we need to realise that *that 'enterprise'-model won't work upside-down*: looking 'up' the stack is like looking upward from the bottom of a well, but looking 'down' the stack needs to take into account the *whole* context – of which the well itself is only one small part. Given that in most large-organisations their big-IT accounts for less than 10% of overall spend – and often a lot less than that – then it should be clear trying to claim as 'enterprise-architecture' an architectural model that can at best only describe perhaps one-tenth of the organisation's concerns is somewhere between laughable and downright dangerous.

Let's be blunt about this: *the real world contains a lot more than just big-IT*. Which means, also bluntly, that the 'BDAT' stack – fundamental to both TOGAF and Archimate, and the basis for Phases B, C and D in the TOGAF ADM – is *misleadingly unusable for anything beyond IT-infrastructure architecture*. Its descriptions even of Information-Systems Architecture, let alone Business-Architecture, are too incomplete and too misleading to be used for anything more than that.

TOGAF metamodel versus real-world

There's quite a nice metamodel in TOGAF 9, and nicely extended in TOGAF 9.1. It's a very nice summary of the entities needed to describe a big-IT infrastructure and its business-context. *But that is all that it can or should be used for*: period. It's usable *solely* for a very small subset of the enterprise: yet what we need – even for a real IT-architecture – must, by definition, be able to describe *anything* in that real-world enterprise. Which, unfortunately, the TOGAF metamodel *actively* prevents us from being able to do.

If you doubt this, try using the TOGAF metamodel to describe any whole-of-context business concern such as security or disaster-recovery, in which human activities and mechanical structures are necessarily 'equal-citizens' alongside the IT-based apps. Try using it to describe the relationships between information about a parcel, versus the parcel itself, in a logistics context where something's gone missing. Try using it to describe the *whole* context for mobile, social, programmable-hardware, an assembly-line, even a data-centre – let alone anything that centres more around physical-machines or people. *It doesn't work*: many if not most of the entities we need simply don't exist in the metamodel – and its arbitrary, unexamined assumptions just get in the way.

In other words, it's yet another darned term-hijack. Frustrating, to say the least...

Predictable-world versus complex-world

The BDAT-stack and the TOGAF metamodel lead inevitably towards an IT-centric architecture. Which is fine, of course, in those specific cases where the IT *is* the centre of concern – but a huge problem when it isn't.

One of the more subtle dangers of IT-centrism – or anything-centrism, actually – is that it tries to remake the world into its own image, constraining our view *of* that wider world. In the case of IT-centrism, the only world it can handle is one that is built around predictable rules and algorithms – a world of *order*, as indicated on the left-hand side of the SCAN frame:

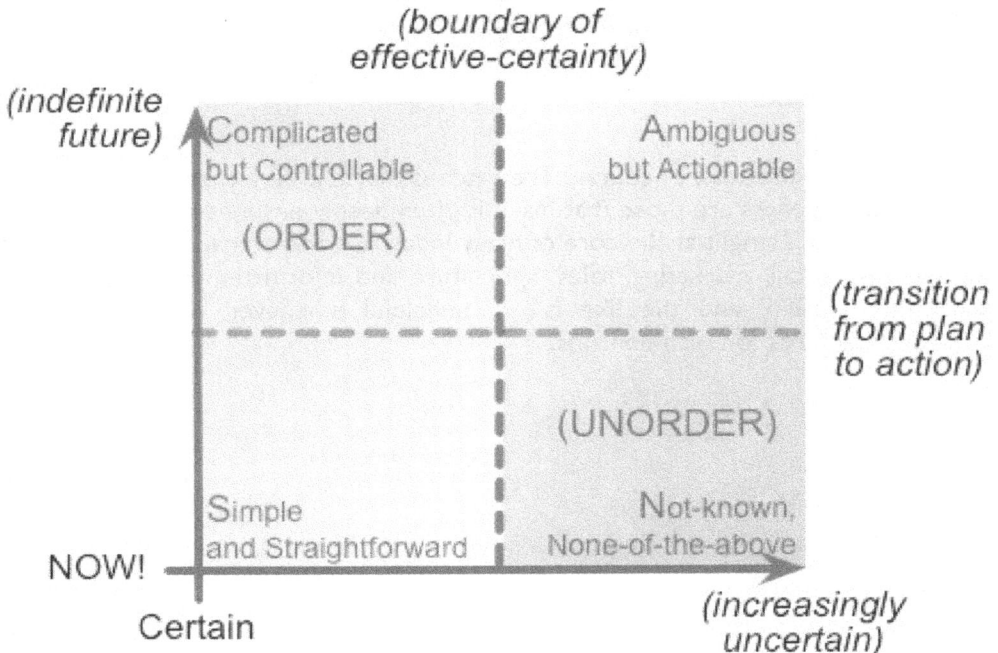

The real-world, however, always includes ambiguities, uncertainties and other forms of *unorder*. Which means that a framework that barely acknowledges even the existence of such things – let alone their real-world prevalence – is inevitably going to be deeply misleading.

More than that, on its own IT can only handle *tame-problems* – problems with a definite true/false answer. The reality, though, is that the real-world consists primarily of 'wild-problems' – of which seemingly-'tame' problems are merely an often-illusory subset, subject to 'variety-weather', 'requisite-fuzziness' and similar deep-uncertainties:

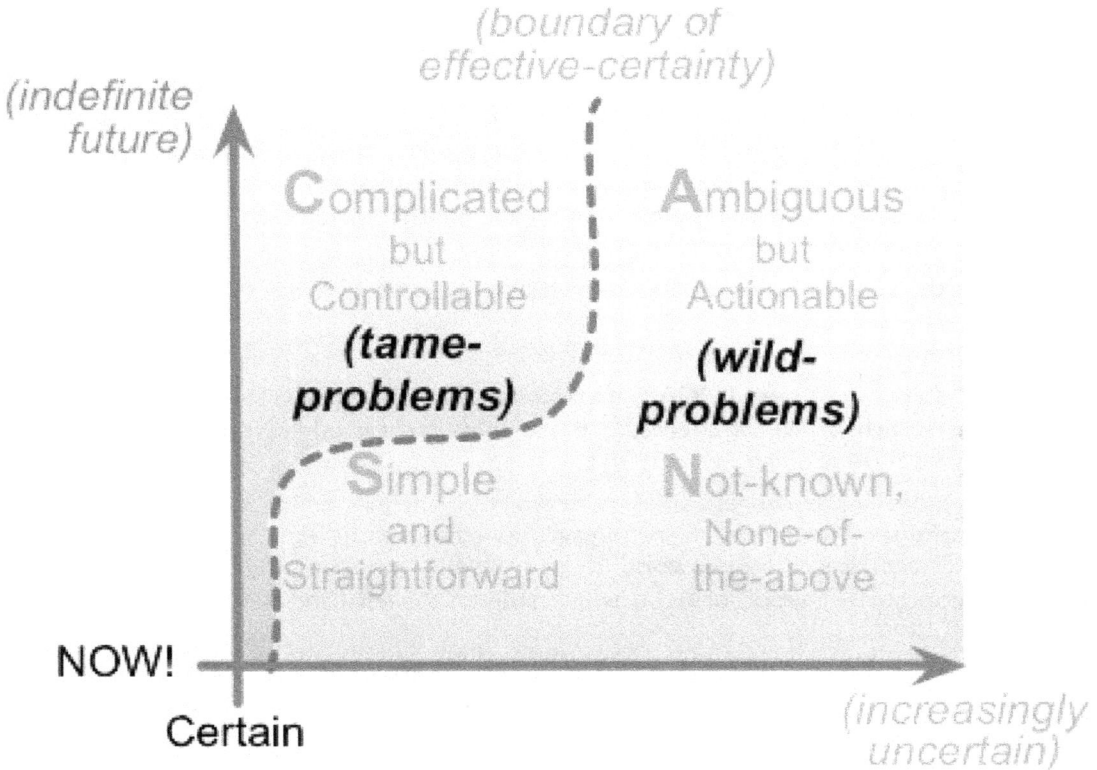

IT is great for mass-sameness, of course. The catch is that the very characteristics that make it great for mass-sameness are those that make it often deeply-unsuited to mass-uniqueness – which, in reality, resides right at the core of many industries and domains, such as healthcare, customer-service, retail, marketing, sales, agriculture and information-search. The inherent IT-centrism of TOGAF and the like is *really* unhelpful whenever we need to develop enterprise-architectures for such domains.

Predefined reference-architectures versus how to create a reference-architecture

Yet another frustration: reference-architectures. At present, the two TOGAF reference-frameworks – TRM and IIIRM – are both so long out-of-date that at one Open Group conference, Allen Brown himself recommended that they should be dropped.

But rather than a mere replacement reference-architecture that will likewise go out of date in a couple of years at most, what we most need instead is advice on *how to create and maintain a reference-architecture* – perhaps using the existing TRM and IIIRM as worked-examples. We also need such reference-architectures to explain their respective 'It depends' constraints and variances – at least to the level of the MoSCoW set, as a minimum.

Yet there's still almost nothing at all on that in the so-called 'standard'. Bah.

Apprentice-level versus journeyman-level

This is another subtle one, though in part it follows directly from the IT-centrism problems above. More specifically, though, it's about where TOGAF and, in particular, TOGAF training sit on the skills-development spectrum:

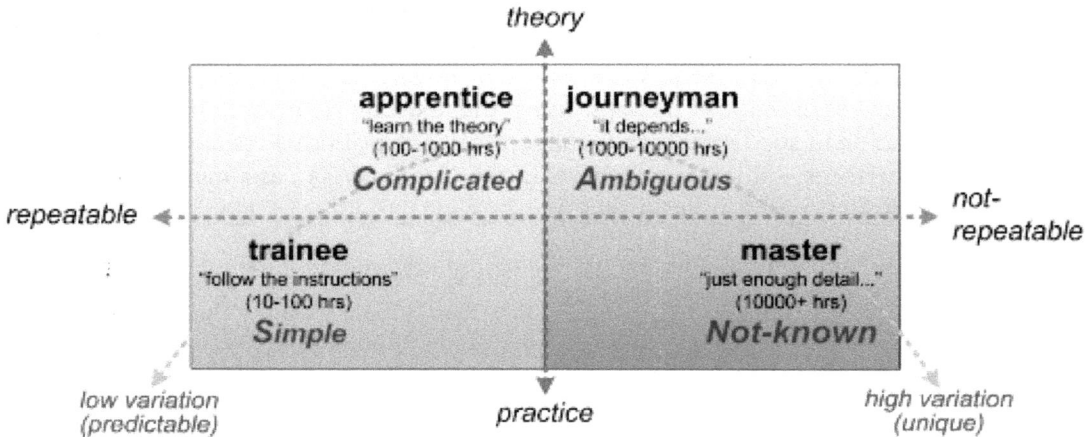

theory

apprentice
"learn the theory"
(100-1000 hrs)
Complicated

journeyman
"it depends..."
(1000-10000 hrs)
Ambiguous

repeatable

not-repeatable

trainee
"follow the instructions"
(10-100 hrs)
Simple

master
"just enough detail..."
(10000+ hrs)
Not-known

low variation (predictable)

practice

high variation (unique)

Where it sits is primarily at the earlier stages of the Apprentice phase, where the learner is just starting to move out of 'follow-the-instructions', and move 'upward' into the first levels of the theory behind those instructions. Yet the focus is still on rote-learning, 'by the book': it's all theory, there's no requirement for real-world practice.

And *without* that grounding in practice, there's a huge, *huge* risk of 'illusory superiority' – delusions of assumed competence that just does not exist in reality. The danger – and I've seen it displayed way too often, on LinkedIn and elsewhere – is that 'newbie' TOGAF trainees have just enough knowledge to get into serious trouble, and nothing like enough knowledge to be able to get out of that trouble on their own, *yet believe that they alone know everything about enterprise-architecture*. In too many cases, the only way to bring such people out of their over-certainties, and on towards the journeyman-level skills that they need for *real-world* enterprise-architecture, is to get them to unlearn every scrap of what they've learnt on their TOGAF course, and start again from scratch. A heck of a waste of effort all round... and a huge frustration in dealing with wave after wave of – let's be blunt – idiots who think they know everything about enterprise-architecture solely because they have a TOGAF certification to wave around. Sigh...

Rote-learning certification versus skills-certification

Certification, ah, <u>certification</u>… probably the biggest bugbear about TOGAF that most of us have in enterprise-architecture, bluntly.

The TOGAF certification comes in two parts: Level 1 (Foundation) and Level 2 (Certified). In essence, Level 1 tests whether the candidate knows the terminology; Level 2 tests knowledge of the full specification.

Both of them are only at a rote-learning level: they can't be more than that, because a TOGAF training-course is only a few days'-worth at most. There's no skills-test at all – and the whole thing is tested via machine-based multiple-choice exam, which is exactly how *not* to test for skills-knowledge.

Given – as above – that several key parts of the TOGAF specification are not merely incomplete but just plain wrong, then all that 'certification' means is that someone has read *wrong* material well enough to pass a multiple-choice exam that has no connection whatsoever to any real-world context.

> (Yes, I do know that Open Group's 'Open-CA' certification *does* require real-world knowledge. TOGAF certification doesn't: it *solely* tests rote-knowledge of *the book itself*, not real-world knowledge – in fact answering the test-questions correctly in terms of real-world practice will often incur a penalty on the test-score. Sigh…)

So in effect, TOGAF certification tests whether you've learnt the content of the book, which itself doesn't connect much or, in some areas, at all, with real-world practice – in other words, not far off a work of wistful fiction. And, starting from that already largely-fictional story, it then demands true/false answers for decision-contexts that in real-world practice are *always* riddled with 'It depends' contextualities. In what possible way could anyone claim that that would be anything other than meaningless, or worse?

Yet various folks still seem kinda uncomfortable about that kind of interpretation:

The certification itself, like any certification, can't mean any more than that [someone has been tested for rote-knowledge], and doesn't purport to.

Correct that it *can't* mean any more than that, and certainly that it *shouldn't*. But given that just about every lazy darn recruiter uses the TOGAF 'certification' as a tick-the-box test not just of purported knowledge but of *competence and skill*, and that Open Group and, even more, its trainer-community actively promote it as such, we *know* that that assertion that "doesn't purport to" is just not true. It's arguable that the implications of that fact are primarily Open Group's problem, not ours – but I really do wish that they'd do something more useful about it than merely trying to silence the critiques and pretend that the problem doesn't exist…

Instead, if perhaps unsurprisingly, Open Group seem very happy about TOGAF certification, as evidenced in this Tweet from a few days ago:

- TOGAF 9 Certification News: Total passes 37,000. Level 1=11445, Level 2=25878 http://ow.ly/DFg6E

And yet I don't know whether to celebrate on their behalf, or weep for the rest of us. The latter, mostly... This supposed success of TOGAF in the marketplace is actually a 'success' that, as we can see from all of the above, is built on exactly how *not* to do 'the architecture of the enterprise' – which means that the *real* mess is getting worse with every passing day. For *everyone's* sake, it really is time that *all* of us should call a halt on the TOGAF hype-machine, and put that bewretched 'EA'-framework back into the IT-only box where it does and must belong.

Okay, you might think that a lot of those complaints above might seem a bit extreme: TOGAF does have *some* value, after all, if only for some specific types of IT-architecture. As one participant in a LinkedIn thread commented:

Let's not throw the baby out with the bathwater

Yet for 'the architecture of the enterprise', turns out there *is* no baby in the TOGAF bathwater – just a rubber duck, a worn-out blob of soap, and a couple of mismatched socks left over from last week's washing. Nothing much that's worth keeping, anyway.

Storm in a bathtub, mostly. But with a *lot* of money riding on it, hence a lot of dollar-laden delusions too.

"*Why* do I loathe thee, TOGAF? Let me count the ways..." Well, that's *some* of the ways and whys, anyway.

Bah.

OREST ROMAN SWYSTUN - SUPERLATIVE TECHNOLOGIES

TOGAF? EA Framework or Not

Part of the challenge in the modern Enterprise Architecture Practice is how difficult it is for the human brain to visualize the intangible virtual assets and processes that interact together and to connect them in a meaningful way. Even in the world of Enterprise Architecture and by applying our own methodologies, practices and frameworks to what we do, we find that the "Enterprise" of Enterprise Architecture is larger than any one "framework". In fact I would go as far as saying that currently we do not have an EA framework. We have many EA frameworks that give us a slice of the picture of the reality or the vision that we are trying to model.

Zachman Framework is probably the most comprehensive, and yet they refer to themselves as an Ontology and not a Framework. Their biggest value comes not from a "framework" but being able to help reify your atomic elements to start understanding how they relate to each other.

The two biggest frameworks that I deal with are DoDAF (Department of Defense Architecture Framework) and TOGAF (The Open Group Architecture Framework). I think as long as the user of said self-proclaimed frameworks realize that these are more guidelines than frameworks they are less likely to have gaps in understanding their Enterprise.

I think that the challenge of Enterprise Architecture is the definition of Enterprise in and of itself. The E can stand for Enterprise (or for that matter everything). Both Enterprise and everything are as easy to define. Both DoDAF and TOGAF attempt to help address that problem. But viewing them singularly and unto themselves is doing Enterprise Architecture a disservice.

58

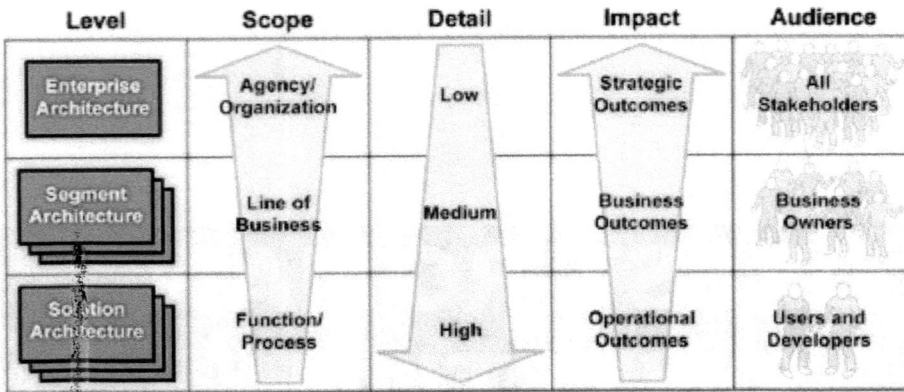

Figure 1-3: Architectural Levels and Attributes

From US OMB the FEA OMB Practice Guidance (above) you can see that Enterprise Architecture is broken down into Segment Architecture and Solution Architecture.

"Segment Architecture defines as a simple roadmap for a core mission area, business service or enterprise service. Segment Architecture is driven by business management and delivers products that improve the delivery of services to citizens and agency staff.

Segment Architecture can consist of Business Architecture, Network Architecture, Data Architecture, Security Architecture, Systems Architecture."

"Solution Architecture defines agency IT assets such as applications or components used to automate and improve individual agency business functions. The scope of a solution architecture is limited to a single project *(or contract)* and is used to implement all or part of a system or business solution."

"By definition, EA is fundamentally concerned with identifying common or shared assets – whether they are strategies, business processes, investments, data, systems or technologies. EA is driven by strategy, it helps an agency identify whether its resources are properly aligned to the agency mission and strategic goals and objectives. From an investment perspective, EA is used to drive decisions about the IT investment portfolio as a whole. Consequently, the primary stakeholders of EA are the senior managers and executives tasked with ensuring the agency fulfills its mission as effectively and efficiently as possible."

Solution Architecture can consist of Business Architecture, Network Architecture, Data Architecture, Security Architecture, Systems Architecture

I would propose that DoDAF and TOGAF are architecture frameworks but they are not EA frameworks. They are a part of the EA framework.

KEVIN LEE SMITH - PRAGMATIC EA

By Kevin Smith (Pragmatic EA**)**
1 January 2018

Introduction

First let me say I am not a TOGAF hater.

Just because I have a negative opinion about something does not mean I hate it. TOGAF, like all frameworks (including POET and PEAF) have good points and bad points. The most fundamental question revolves around the domain that a framework has been designed to mature. And let's not forget a framework is something that helps people improve (we prefer to say mature) HOW something is done.

If you use a framework designed to mature one domain (say Project management e.g. PRINCE2) to mature a different domain (say Service Management) you are probably not going to get the results you were hoping for.

So, when I say "TOGAF is NOT an EA framework", I say so in the same way that "I say PRINCE2 is NOT an EA Framework". However, I don't say that about PRINCE2 because there is not an army of people saying PRINCE2 is an EA framework. On the other hand there is an army saying (and have been saying for many years) that TOGAF is an EA Framework. Imagine how confused Service Management would be if people had been saying for many years the PRINCE2 is a service management framework and ITIL never got a look-in! This is why I say that TOGAF has done more to damage the EA profession (such as it is) than anything else on the planet.

The rest of this section, comprises all the information (contained in POET and PEAF) that relates to explaining why TOGAF is NOT an EA Framework.

Theory and Complexity

Context > Where POET and PEAF Fit > Theory & Complexity

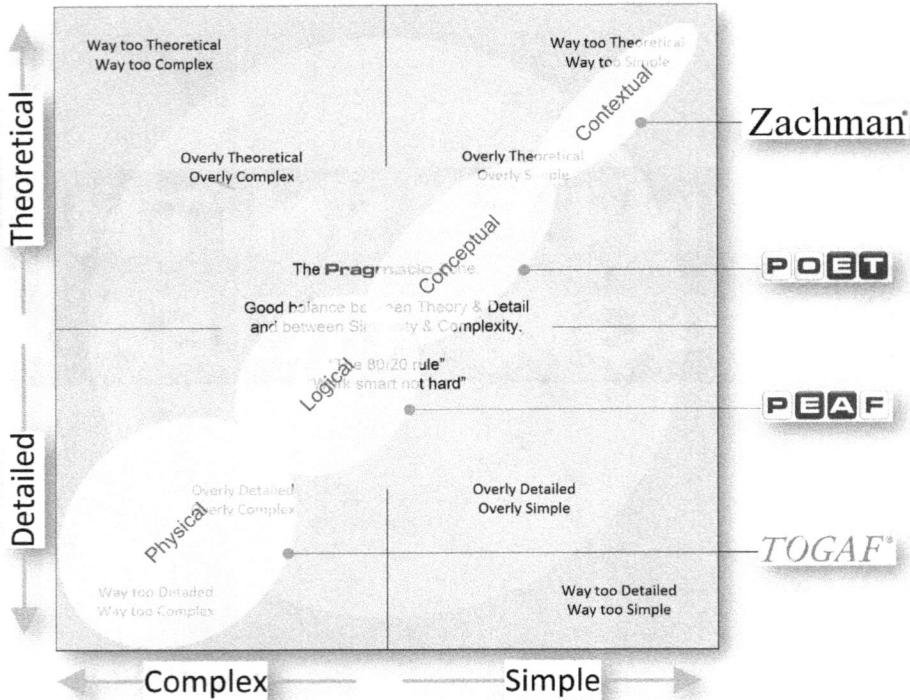

© Pragmatic EA Ltd (2008-2016)

Here we present a method of categorising frameworks and ontologies.

The vertical axis ranges between the Theoretical and the Detailed, while the horizontal axis ranges between the Simple and the Complex.

The green area illustrates a domain of balance between these extremes, where the 80/20 rule applies and a good balance between simplicity and complexity and between theory and detail is achieved.

The red area illustrates a range where these categorisations stray too far into extremes and the opposite of the 80/20 rule applies.

The blue area illustrates a range between these points.

◆ **Zachman** is an Ontology and is therefore Simple & Theoretical. However, it could be said that it is too Simple and too Theoretical to enable easy adoption. It effectively provides Contextual guidance.

◆ **TOGAF** is very Detailed and Complex. It could be said that it is too complex and too detailed to enable easy adoption. It effectively provides Physical guidance.

There is a noticeable chasm between them.

- ◆ **POET** is an Ontology and therefore by definition tends towards the theoretical like Zachman. However, POET is less theoretical than Zachman with an appropriate level of complexity to make it easily usable. **Zachman and POET do not compete.** They are complementary to each other. It is not a question of Zachman or POET but more a question of Zachman and POET. It effectively provides Conceptual guidance.

- ◆ **PEAF** is a Framework and therefore, by definition, tends towards the Concrete like TOGAF. However, PEAF is less concrete with an appropriate level of complexity to make it easily usable. **PEAF and TOGAF do not compete.** They are complementary to each other. It is not a question of PEAF or TOGAF but more a question of PEAF and TOGAF. It effectively provides Logical guidance.

In this way, POET and PEAF bridge the chasm between Zachman and TOGAF.

Zachman, TOGAF, ITIL, COBIT, PEAF

Context > Where POET and PEAF Fit > Zachman, TOGAF, ITIL, COBIT, PEAF

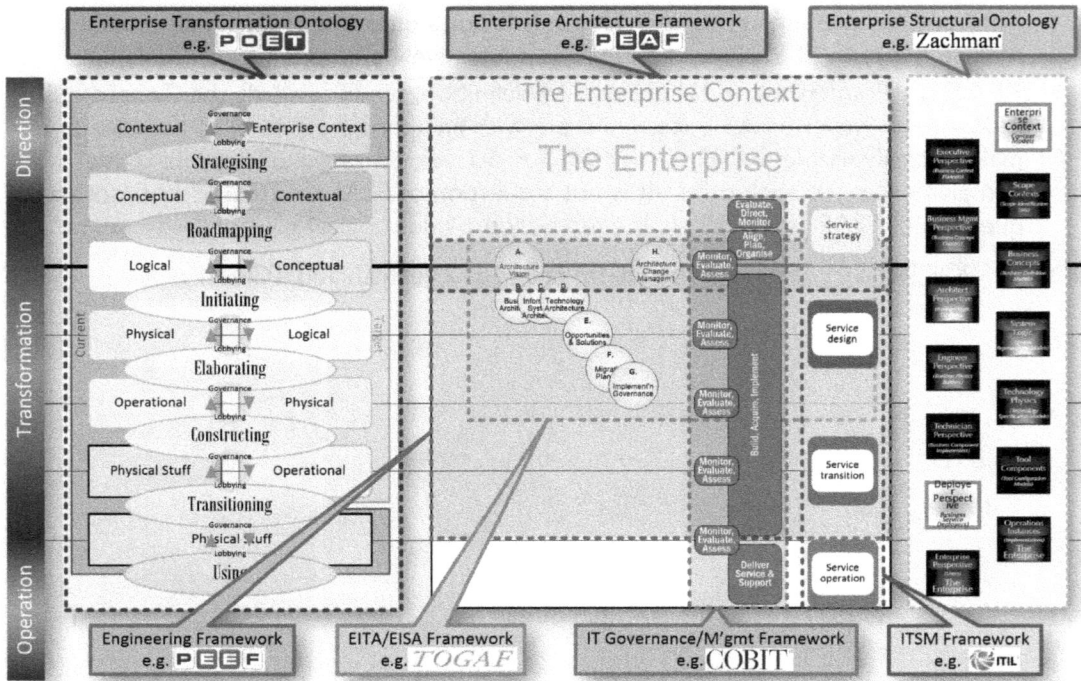

© Pragmatic EA Ltd (2008-2016)

Here we show how other frameworks map on to the Transformation cascade (From strategy to Deployment) that POET defines.

The Enterprise Context consists of all the things that are not part of The Enterprise (i.e. not directly under its control) but affect or is affected in some way by it. Things like Customers, Suppliers, Partners, Regulators, etc.

The thick black line across the diagram marks the delineation between Project Portfolio Planning above and Project Execution below.

The ellipses of POET show the phases of transformation while the rounded boxes show the models used. The boxes with square black lines are not models but actually physical things. All models are shown to exist in two fundamental states, Current and Target. There are also, of course, intermediate states but they are not shown to aid readability.

In between each phase of transformation, we show the Governance and Lobbying disciplines of POET (using Enterprise Debt™) which, as you will see later, is the key to making the whole coherent, connected and aligned.

Zachman®

Zachman maps almost one-to-one to POET's structural and transformational levels although we also show the missing Perspective and Model.

It should also be noted that this mapping is only general as there are other anomalies such as Zachman's Architect and Engineer perspectives (shown in Yellow and Green) which are actually fundamental perspectives which occur at all levels not just at one.

TOGAF®

TOGAF is mostly a Project IT Architecture (PITA) framework for two reasons:

- ♦ **Vertically** although it includes some Roadmapping it is mainly concerned with projects.
- ♦ **Horizontally** the blue box is shown to not cover the entire width of the Enterprise because TOGAF's domain is really only IT. It does cover things that are not IT, such as processes and business things, but only where these business things have some relationship or connection to IT. Consequently, there are other things in the Enterprise, that do not use IT, that TOGAF ignores.

ITIL®

ITIL in its original form only covered the Service Operation or Management area but over recent years has grown up the transformation stack although its domain is still only really IT Services.

COBIT®

COBIT covers four main domains:

- ♦ Evaluate Direct, Monitor **(EDM)** and Align, Plan Organise **(APO)** map to the Management domain of the Roadmapping level of POET.
- ♦ Build, Acquire, Implement **(BAI)** maps to the Management domain of the Roadmapping Initiating, Elaborating, Constructing and Transitioning levels of POET.
- ♦ Monitor, Evaluate, Assess **(MEA)** maps to the Governance domain/interface between the Roadmapping Initiating, Elaborating, Constructing Transitioning and Using levels of POET.
- ♦ Deliver Service & Support **(DSO)** maps to the Using domain of the Operation/Support domains of DOTS.

PEAF™

PEAF is an Enterprise Architecture Framework for two reasons:

- ♦ **Vertically** - it covers the Strategising and Roadmapping phases and is therefore concerned more with strategic cross-project things rather than tactical project-specific things. It is concerned with projects a little, but only from the EA Governance perspective - down to projects and Lobbying up from Projects - This is where the concept of Enterprise Debt™ comes in that you will see later.
- ♦ **Horizontally** - it covers the entire enterprise including but NOT LIMITED to IT.

PEEF™

PEEF is an Enterprise Engineering Framework for two reasons:

- ♦ **Vertically** - it covers the Initiating to Transitioning phases and is therefore concerned more with tactical project-specific things rather than strategic cross-project things. It is concerned with the entirety of projects.
- ♦ **Horizontally** - it covers the entire enterprise including but NOT LIMITED to IT.

Framework Comparison

Environment > Frameworks > Comparison > Criteria

Strategic	Transformational Focus
Project	How much the framework is focussed on Strategic Planning and Roadmapping vs Project Level work.
Enterprise	Structural Focus
IT	How much the framework is focussed on the structure of the entire Enterprise vs mostly IT.
Detail	Content
Usability	An indication of how detailed the framework is vs how usable it is.

© Pragmatic EA Ltd (2008-2016)

Here we see some criteria that we will use to analyse and compare PEAF, TOGAF and Zachman:

Transformational Focus

♦ **Strategic** - Frameworks that score highly here are ones whose remit is more towards the Strategising, Roadmapping and governance of Initiating phases of the Transformation domain - the domains typically associated with Enterprise Architecture.

♦ **Project** - Frameworks that score highly here are ones whose remit is more towards the Initiating, Elaborating, and the governance of Construction phases of the Transformation domain - the domains typically associated with Enterprise Engineering.

Structural Focus

♦ **Enterprise** - Frameworks that score highly here are ones whose remit is more towards the structure of the entire Enterprise without limitation - the domain typically associated with Enterprise Architecture.

♦ **IT** - Frameworks that score highly here are ones whose remit is more towards the structure of only those parts of the Enterprise consisting of IT and the other parts of the Enterprise that are connected to IT in some way - the domain typically associated with Enterprise IT Architecture (EITA).

Content

♦ **Detail** - Frameworks that score highly here are ones that are large and contain massive amounts of detail.

♦ **Usability** - Frameworks that score highly here are ones that are easy to understand, use and deploy.

Here we see the raw scores for each framework.

Of course you may have different views and can use the Framework Comparison Toolkit Spreadsheet in PEAF to modify them as you wish with a resulting changing of overall scores.

	TOGAF	Zachman	PEAF
Strategic	2	8	10
Project	5	8	2
Enterprise	2	2	10
IT	10	10	10
Detail	8	1	4
Usability	1	1	10
Total	28	30	46

© Pragmatic EA Ltd (2008-2016)

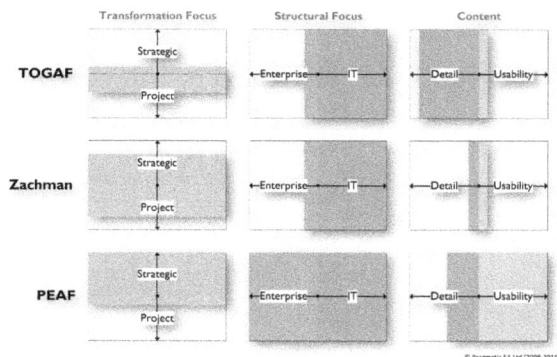

© Pragmatic EA Ltd (2008-2016)

And here we see the same information represented in a graphical style

TOGAF

TOGAF's Transformational focus is mainly on the Initiating and Elaboration phases of projects and the governance of Construction. It does cover Roadmapping to a small degree but only really from the point of roadmapping for a very large project or a program. It doesn't cover Construction or Transitioning and its Structural focus is very IT oriented. It does provide a large amount of detail but largely because of this and other issues it is not very usable and difficult to implement.

Zachman

♦ Zachman's Transformational focus is largely strategic in nature and does cover most of the project domain but is very IT oriented. It doesn't provide much detail at all and not much guidance on how to use it either.

PEAF

♦ PEAF's Transformational focus is on the Strategising, Roadmapping and Governance of the Initiating phases of the Transformation domain. Structurally it includes IT but is not limited to IT, instead covering the entire Enterprise domain. It offers a moderate amount of detail and concentrates mostly on the fundamentals that Enterprises need to get right. Because of this it is extremely usable and provides a lot of help to implement it - The Adoption section - which constitutes the Maturity Model.

66

Even if you accept the raw scores provided by PEAF or change them, you may also place a different emphasis on each category, favouring some more than others. This will also change the resultant scores.

Here we see how the scores change if you make **Project** level guidance and **Detail** your preference.

	Weighting	TOGAF	Zachman	PEAF
Strategic	5%	0.1	0.4	0.5
Project	40%	2	3.2	0.8
Enterprise	5%	0.1	0.1	0.5
IT	5%	0.5	0.5	0.5
Detail	40%	3.2	0.4	1.6
Usability	5%	0.05	0.05	0.5
Total	100%	5.95	4.65	4.4

© Pragmatic EA Ltd (2008-2010)

	Weighting	TOGAF	Zachman	PEAF
Strategic	30%	0.6	2.4	3
Project	10%	0.5	0.8	0.2
Enterprise	10%	0.2	0.2	1
IT	10%	1	1	1
Detail	10%	0.8	0.1	0.4
Usability	30%	0.3	0.3	3
Total	100%	3.4	4.8	8.6

© Pragmatic EA Ltd (2008-2010)

Here we see how the scores change if you make **Strategic** level guidance and **Usability** your preference.

ABDENOUR BOUATELI

Email Comment

This topic is very important.

Effectively, some people said that TOGAF is an Enterprise Architecture.

I am not sure because an EA Framework is focused only on IS transition at different levels such as Business, information, applicative and technical Architecture.

But, when you address a problematic of an Enterprise in the global, i think an Information system is just one part and you need to take an Enterprise With others parts such as an organization , suppliers, segmentation client, product, strategy, ...etc.

Where TOGAF is huge and Zachman is chiefly a taxonomy, PEAF cuts to the heart of what is needed to begin reaping the benefits of Enterprise Architecture. More than just a classification scheme or descriptive content, it provides a toolkit consisting of the vision, communication materials, maturity matrix, risks, plans, Metamodel, principles, processes and metrics required to hit the ground running.

For example, PEAF has been formulated over a large number of years by understanding what works and what does not work in a pragmatic sense.

PEAF provides a quick start toolkit necessary to begin and sustain an Enterprise Architecture programme of work for organisations seeking to infuse and reap the benefits EA can bring.

GRAHAM BERRISFORD - AVANCIER LTD

LinkedIn Message

TOGAF 7 was an IT architecture framework. TOGAF 8 moved closer to being an EA framework, but TOGAF 9 moved away again, including more guidance at the solution architecture level. It has become a generalised management framework for any kind of "architecture project". It is not prescriptive. Users are expected to tailor the method, selecting those parts relevant to their work, and melding into their local programme/project method..

APPENDIX

Sources

- ◆ Book cover: Tropical Storm Lee - NASA/NOAA GOES Project Science Team.
- ◆ Technical Debt - www.wikipedia.org/wiki/Technical_debt
- ◆ Zachman Framework - www.wikipedia.org/wiki/Zachman_Framework
- ◆ TOGAF (The Open Group Architecture Framework) - www.opengroup.org/togaf/
- ◆ Business Motivation Model - www.omg.org/spec/BMM/
- ◆ Enhanced Business Motivation Model - www.MotivationModel.com
- ◆ ITIL (IT Infrastructure Library) - www.itil-officialsite.com
- ◆ COBIT (Control Objectives for Information and Related Technology) - www.wikipedia.org/wiki/Cobit

Resources

- ◆ The **Pragmatic EA** website (www.PragmaticEA.com) is the official source for all PF[2] related materials.